CULTURE AND VALUES AT THE HEART OF POLICY MAKING
An Insider's Guide

Stephen Muers

T0324019

First published in Great Britain in 2020 by

Policy Press
University of Bristol
1-9 Old Park Hill
Bristol
BS2 8BB
UK
t: +44 (0)117 954 5940
pp-info@bristol.ac.uk
www.policypress.co.uk

© Policy Press 2020

British Library Cataloguing in Publication Data
A catalogue record for this book is available from the British Library.

ISBN 978-1-4473-5615-8 paperback
ISBN 978-1-4473-5617-2 ePub
ISBN 978-1-4473-5616-5 ePdf

Cover design by Robin Hawes
Front cover image: iStock/Galore777
Printed and bound in Great Britain by CMP, Poole
Policy Press uses environmentally responsible print partners

To Jane and Robin, who taught me about
culture and values in all their forms

Contents

About the author

Stephen Muers has held a range of senior policy-making and strategy roles in the public and non-profit sectors. These have included positions in the Cabinet Office, the Ministry of Justice, the Department of Energy and Climate Change and the Prime Minister's Strategy Unit, and as non-executive director of an NHS Trust. He is currently Head of Strategy and Market Development at Big Society Capital, a trustee of the Friends Provident Foundation and a Policy Fellow at the Institute for Policy Research, University of Bath.

Acknowledgements

The ideas that formed this book began to come together during two days I spent at the University of Bath in April 2016 as a Policy Fellow at the Institute for Policy Research. Professor Nick Pearce, Director of the Institute, has been an invaluable source of advice and support throughout the long subsequent journey towards creating this book. I would never have reached this point without his input.

I have drawn on many different experiences from my time as a policy maker, and owe debts of insight to too many colleagues to mention. However, my two periods in the Prime Minister's Strategy Unit (PMSU) were particularly important both in shaping my thinking and in providing an extraordinary network of talented people who care about public policy. So I am especially grateful to the PMSU alumni, especially Gavin Kelly (with whom I worked on the public value paper discussed in Chapter 3) and David Knott (my co-author on the paper I mention in the Introduction). Owain Service and David Halpern were both fantastic colleagues during that period and also kind enough to invite me to present my emerging ideas to the Behavioural Insights Team.

Will Paxton at Kivu International is another ex-colleague from the PMSU and provided me with some invaluable insights into the international development literature as well as the example from the recent Sri Lankan election mentioned in Chapter 11. I am also grateful for the opportunity he arranged for me to discuss my ideas with the wider Kivu team.

Some of the ideas in this book were trailed in my essay in the collection *Radical Visions for a Future Government*, published by Nesta in 2019. I'm grateful to Tom Symons and the rest of the Nesta team for the opportunity to test some thinking in that format.

The team at Policy Press – Laura Vickers-Rendall, Amelia Watts-Jones and Millie Prekop – have been everything that a first-time author could wish for: professional, encouraging, clear and easy to work with.

I have been lucky to have close friends who have always been prepared to indulge me in debating politics and policy issues, in the process sharpening my thinking as well as having fun. In this group I would particularly like to thank Steve Siddals, Thomas Carter, Simon James, Sarah Donaldson and Mike Goldby.

Finally, I owe the greatest thanks of all to Olivia and Marcus, without whose love and companionship writing a book would feel neither worthwhile nor possible.

Introduction

In 2007 I was working for the Prime Minister's Strategy Unit, part of the Cabinet Office in London. The Labour Party had been in a strong position in government for ten years, with large majorities in Parliament and weak opposition. As he came towards the end of his time as Prime Minister, Tony Blair initiated a 'policy review', a process that aimed to look at the achievements of his government and suggest directions for the future.

I was in charge of the section of this review looking at public services – health, education, criminal justice and so on. Improving these services had been a top priority for the Blair government. It had implemented major reform programmes, backed by increasing expenditure on health care in particular. It had set up the Delivery Unit, headed by Michael Barber, to bring to bear new ways of tracking and improving performance. Every year the Queen's Speech at the opening of the new Parliamentary year had heralded new legislation to reform the National Health Service, or schools, or childcare or other public services.

However, when government ministers gathered together as part of the policy review process to reflect on what they had achieved, my fellow officials and I heard an overwhelming sense of frustration. Minister after minister felt that nothing much had changed. While resource pressures in some areas had been eased, the fundamental dynamics of many services were very familiar from before they came to power. In particular, they were frustrated that large inequalities in health outcomes, educational attainment and vulnerability to crime had proved very hard to shift. For a progressive government like this one, that felt like failure. And as ministers talked about these frustrations, the concept that came up time and time again was 'culture'. The culture of the public service agencies, and the culture of the communities they served, were so strong and deep-seated that the best reform programmes, backed up by money and expertise, couldn't compete.

As a result of this strong message from our political masters, my colleague David Knott and I wrote a paper about culture change and how government could think about it. In retrospect this was a rather peculiar and abstract piece for two civil servants to write and publish on a government website, but the Strategy Unit in that period was given an unusual degree of latitude. We concluded that while thinking about culture and how to change it was hard, and didn't easily fit into many of the frameworks employed by policy makers, some of the challenges that government faced would be insoluble without it.

Fast-forward nearly a decade, and everyone with an interest in politics, policy and social change was desperately looking for explanations for the unexpected (by most) votes in the United Kingdom to leave the European Union and in the United States to elect Donald Trump as President. Many commentators focused on the stagnant real incomes experienced by middle-income workers since the 2008 financial crash (and indeed before, in some cases), and on the increase in wealth held by the most well-off. However, another school of argument, much of which I found compelling, identified cultural factors and deep-seated values as crucial drivers of support for Trump and Brexit. I will discuss some of this work in more detail in Chapter 6.

In between these two periods, as I continued to work in a range of roles around the public sector, I became increasingly focused on a third phenomenon that pushed me to place culture and values at the centre of my understanding. This was repeated failures of accountability. On a macro level, like everyone else I saw the leaders of huge financial institutions make catastrophic misjudgements, with supposedly independent advisors in the accountancy and legal professions, as well as non-executive directors representing shareholders, doing nothing to check them. Virtually none of the individuals involved faced any meaningful sanctions. At a micro level, I saw senior civil servants and ministers responsible for failed projects and misguided policies that wasted money and harmed citizens facing no damage to their careers. There appeared to be a disjunction between what was needed for personal advancement and what was needed to make policy that actually worked. And yet this was happening in an advanced democracy with, on paper, all the tools of accountability: a credible independent court system, a fully independent National Audit Office (NAO), Parliamentary scrutiny committees, a well-resourced, reasonably diverse and institutionally sceptical media. I concluded that culture once again had a major part to play. This was through both the culture and values of the institutions in which accountability was meant to work, but perhaps more importantly the way in which cultural norms and values-based actions play out in the political system act to undermine much of the machinery of accountability that we have built.

This book is an attempt to weave these experiences and observations about the importance of culture and values into a coherent whole, and to draw some conclusions for how to do public policy better as a result. I have broken the argument into three sections.

Chapter 1 introduces the concepts of culture and values as I will use them in the book. Part One, Chapters 2 to 5, sets out why culture and values matter when making decisions about public policy. They matter for four main reasons. First, culture affects outcomes. This is probably the least surprising claim I make in the book, as it is both intuitive and well evidenced in literature from all sorts of settings. However, the way in which it does so, in particular by focusing our attention on the culture and values of those implementing policy at the front line rather than decision makers in Whitehall or Washington, is vital for understanding the rest of the argument and some of the proposed solutions. Second, a policy needs to be legitimate, both for it to succeed on its own terms and because legitimacy is a good thing in itself, and what is legitimate in a given society is dependent on the values that its members hold. Third, many of the questions that we ask the political and policy process to resolve are values-based, and it is only through engaging with the value judgements that people make that we can hope to come to a satisfactory solution. In fact, confusion about when something is an argument about values and when it isn't creates a lot of commonly seen problems in conversations about politics. Finally in this part, governments affect culture and values by their actions, intentionally or not. Given that this effect exists, it seems to me wilfully short-sighted not to consider it explicitly when making decisions.

Part Two, Chapters 6 and 7, looks at how the importance of culture and values affect our political system and the way that policy is made overall. It sets out that it is rational in principle for voters to act on the basis of values, and that there is strong evidence that they do so in practice. At this point I come back to the implications for accountability, showing how this model of voter choice means that many of the ways we expect decision makers in a democracy to be held to account are doomed to failure. Rather than looking at whether a decision has good or bad consequences and then deciding their view of the decision maker accordingly, most of the time people decide whether they like the decision maker and interpret a range of partial and messy facts to fit with that prior judgement. This part concludes by suggesting some different approaches to accountability to deal with the problem described above, by focusing more on real-time front-line feedback on services and on interrogating the values-base of political decisions.

Part Three, Chapters 8 to 11, looks at ways I think we should adapt policy making to better reflect the centrality of culture. One is to take the power of symbolic action in policy making seriously, and to apply the same rigour and professionalism around it that we do to other disciplines like cost-benefit analysis. Secondly, I discuss how decentralising power over policy making and delivery can help respond to some of the challenges raised earlier in the argument. Thirdly, I look at how organisations can embody values, and when building new organisations is the best tool to bring about a desired shift. In the final chapter I discuss how evidence and the movement towards 'evidence-based policy making' should be seen in the light of a focus on culture, and where and how evidence can be useful.

As I set out at the start of this introduction, the inspiration for the arguments in this book comes mainly from my own experience as a practitioner and rather obsessive observer of the policy process. However, I have also drawn on some significant areas of academic research. I use elements of a longstanding tradition of work on why implementation of policy is a messy and non-linear process (sometimes called complexity theory, or implementation theory). The section on how culture and values affect the political system in particular is influenced by the emerging 'realist' school of democratic theory, as well as extensive empirical work on the drivers of political choice. I would encourage readers to delve more deeply into those fields, where they will find levels of nuance and sophistication well beyond a short book like this one. The section on practical ways to adapt policy making is less grounded in academic work and more in practical experience. Partly for that reason, and also in the spirit of the recommendations themselves, it is necessarily somewhat tentative. It is only by trying some of the directions I suggest, getting them wrong, learning and trying again, that any progress will occur. That is what I will be trying to do, and I encourage you to join me on that journey.

1

What are culture and values?

The experiences that I set out in the Introduction do not have immediately obvious connections. Why are the same concepts – culture and values – useful for analysing such different phenomena as the difficulty of reforming the National Health Service under Tony Blair's government and the election victory of Donald Trump? There is a risk that 'culture' and 'values' are both abstract and potentially woolly terms, which don't have enough bite to them to drive real understanding. Therefore this first chapter sets out what I mean by culture and values. There are several different concepts in play here, and understanding how they differ will be important to the arguments in the following chapters. It is also vital to see how they are connected. In reality the ways policy makers, organisations that interact with policy, and individual citizens act stem from a mixture of cultural and value-driven factors, as well as other elements. That mixture depends on the specific situation and the wider context, and disentangling its separate elements is not always practically possible or useful.

There are three elements to the concepts of culture and values as used in this book. They are:

- the set of written and (especially) unwritten rules that define the institutions within which people operate and which enable them to work together with each other and with wider society;
- the set of beliefs about how the world works and about ethical principles like fairness and justice that affect how policy is made and implemented; and

- the set of practical and psychological shortcuts that everyone uses to navigate complexity and incomplete information.

Each of these elements operates at two levels: the level of policy makers themselves and the level of society as a whole (see Table 1.1).[1] It is the interaction of all the elements at both levels that creates the environment of culture and values that I discuss in the rest of the book.

Table 1.1: Examples of culture and values

	Unwritten rules of conduct	Ethical beliefs	Dealing with complexity
Policy makers	Example: acceptable language in political debate	Example: priority given to reducing inequality	Example: assumptions about human motivation
Society as a whole	Example: expectations of mutual support in times of hardship	Example: acceptable forms of family relationships	Example: stories and myths used to explain history

Unwritten rules in institutions and society

The first of these elements will be familiar to anyone who has worked in a large organisation. There is a set of rules about how things can and can't be done: which group makes which decisions, who signs off expenditure, how new employees are recruited. There is then a set of unwritten rules that are often more powerful in deciding what an organisation can achieve. These unwritten rules cover things like style in speaking and writing, what approaches that are technically allowed under the rules but are in fact unacceptable (or vice versa), and what people trust one another to do without formal approvals or scrutiny. Institutions that make and deliver public policy carry these unwritten rules just like any others. The important point to recognise is that those unwritten rules, which are a type of culture, affect policy outcomes.

Some of the most powerful evidence for this assertion comes from the work of Elinor Ostrom (2000, 2009). She took on the classic public policy challenge of the collective action problem and the risk of the 'tragedy of the commons': how do communities manage common resources when the economic incentive for individuals is to deplete the resource as far as possible? At the risk of greatly simplifying her extremely sophisticated body of work, one important conclusion is that institutional culture, and particularly levels of trust, are extremely important. High levels of trust enable societies to achieve an equilibrium where common resources are not depleted and everyone benefits. Such an equilibrium requires trust and strong norms of behaviour operating within both policy institutions and wider society, and also between them. Take the example of managing fish stocks, a classic collective action problem. Each fish that one boat catches is one less for all the others to pursue. If everyone catches as much as they can, there will soon be no fish left and everyone suffers. To achieve a more positive outcome, fishermen need to trust one another to report their catches honestly and stick to agreed quotas. Fisheries regulators need to trust one another not to take bribes to turn a blind eye to excess catches or to set quotas in a way that favours particular localities or industry groups. The boat operators in turn need to trust the regulators to treat everyone fairly and listen to legitimate concerns that they raise, while the regulators need to trust the operators to tell the truth about what they catch and what they see happening to the development of fish stocks. A strong culture of trust, honesty and following accepted norms enables an effective policy outcome.

Ostrom (2000) also argues that trust alone will not be enough to sustain a culture of constructive cooperation. She says that it will also be important to have a system whereby those monitoring the relevant social norms (the fishing regulators in this example) are accountable to the wider society. If they are not accountable, the particular policy system can evolve an equilibrium that works for those involved but not for anyone else. To extend the fishing example, imagine a case where the regulator and the boat operators have agreed (informally) a schedule of bribes that the operators will pay the regulator to turn a blind eye to infringements of the rules. This could lead to a sustainable system, if the bribes required for egregious over-fishing are high enough. However, the rest of society suffers, as new entrants to the industry are excluded by the arrangements and more broadly bribe-taking becomes normalised, with wider negative consequences.

Of course, the opposite to a high-trust high-accountability equilibrium is possible. Different cultural environments with lower levels of trust can lead to very different outcomes. A good example to illustrate this is the experience of Southern Italy. Calabria (roughly the toes and instep of the Italian boot) is stunningly beautiful. From towns like Pizzo and Tropea, the views across the Tyrrhenian Sea to Stromboli and the other small islands off the Sicilian coast are sensational. However, there is another side to those towns, and even more to the larger cities like Reggio Calabria. This other side is the ubiquitous rubbish, poorly maintained or indeed half-finished buildings, and the terrible state of many public spaces. Those 'commons' that Ostrom talks about are certainly suffering. Many scholars have argued that a lack of social trust lies behind the set of cultural norms that lead to this situation. Fukuyama (2014) pulls together a series of studies that point to low levels of trust in public institutions and civil society and a culture of cynicism towards any initiative that claims to promote a form of common good. Putnam (1993) provides strong empirical evidence of low levels of civic engagement in Southern Italy and what Fukuyama (2014: 110) calls 'long-standing inherited cultural values' in the region that explain many of the struggles it continues to have with managing common resources. He argues that the weak trust in institutions which undermines the management of common resources has its roots in feudal rule in Southern Italy, which persisted much later than in many other parts of Europe.

Trust is one very important part of institutional and social culture, and an excellent example for showing why it matters. It is not the only component and is used here simply as an illustration. As we consider different elements of the political and policy-making system in the following chapters, different unwritten organisational rules will emerge as playing a significant role.

Value systems

The second element of culture and values is less immediately obvious. We can all recognise the culture of institutions we work in. But values sit deeper and are generally less overt in policy-making conversations. I can illustrate this from my own experience. In my role on the Investment Committee at Big Society Capital I have been part of deciding how to allocate investment capital to deliver social benefit in the United Kingdom. We had a set of frameworks for considering social impact and looking at whether the funds we were investing in had good systems for considering it. What became obvious, however, is that the frameworks provided a surface structure for the discussions but really many of our debates about social impact were profoundly value-driven and much less amenable to analytical tools. What kinds of social benefit do we care more about? Is it better to go for deep impact on a few people or broad impact on a large number? Understanding how each individual's ethical values affect our judgements helps us have clearer and more honest conversations (Muers, 2017). Public policy is often concerned with similar ethical questions, and therefore understanding where personal moral judgements come into play and how to handle them at an institutional or society-wide level is essential. Chapter 4 discusses in more detail how policy making and political systems need to accommodate values and help to resolve situations where they clash.

Ethical judgements about right and wrong are one part of the value systems that we all hold. Another part is our deep-seated assumptions about how the world works. By deep-seated assumptions I mean going beyond beliefs about specific events or policy issues to more fundamental factors, like whether people are fundamentally motivated by money or whether the world operates in a predictable way or is more chaotic. Policy makers need to be aware of the differences between such world-views and how they affect the way people engage with policy questions. When I was a senior civil servant in the UK government I once had a Secretary of State who approached every issue from the perspective of economic incentives.

What financial gains or losses would people make in different situations? How should we, as the policy department, structure rewards and penalties for the various service providers we worked with to get the outcome we wanted? The department spent a lot of time analysing costs and benefits and focusing on commercial contract terms that would reward or penalise particular behaviour.

After a Cabinet reshuffle we greeted a new Secretary of State, and rapidly discovered he thought very differently. His view of the world revolved around leadership. He framed many policy choices by thinking about who would or should be able to take which decisions in a system, and how the best leaders could be found and then enabled to do the things he felt were most important. These two were from the same political party, and shared many ideological positions and policy goals. But we had to change the whole way we were thinking as a result of the shifting world-view at the top.

To put this example from my experience into a theoretical framework that explains why moral values and world-views are relevant to the policy-making process, we can turn to the work of Paul Sabatier (Sabatier and Jenkins-Smith, 1999). His 'Advocacy Coalition Framework' is a sophisticated account of how groups of actors in the policy process come together and interact with one another and with exogenous factors to create policy change. The crucial point from our perspective here is his argument, based on empirical evidence from several case studies, that values and world-views play a key role in forming such coalitions. He says that advocacy coalitions are formed of people that 'share a set of normative and causal beliefs' (Sabatier and Jenkins-Smith, 1999: 120). This includes both of the two elements identified as part of 'values': beliefs about right and wrong and also beliefs about how causation works in the world at a fundamental level. My two Secretaries of State were probably in agreement on many normative values, coming as they did from similar places on the political and ideological spectrum. However, their views of the underlying causal drivers of policy outcomes made them interpret policy challenges very differently, demanding both different styles of analysis and different recommendations.

Navigating complexity

Trust, values and world-views are profound questions that go to the heart of human behaviour, in policy making and elsewhere. They differ widely between people. The third element of culture, however, is less deep and more common to all of us. This element is the outcome of the ways in which all humans have to navigate a complex unpredictable world. Such methods of navigation are as important for understanding the overall collection of norms, habits and behaviours that I will call 'culture' in the rest of this book as the other elements set out above.

The psychology of decision making, especially in an economic or policy-making context, is a popular topic at the moment. Scholars increasingly recognise that the 'economic man' rational-choice models of the classical economics textbooks or the public choice school of public policy theory are inherently unrealistic and do not reflect the way in which people actually make decisions. A joint report by the Behavioural Insight Team and the Institute for Government (Hallsworth et al, 2018) gives an excellent review of the way that psychological shortcuts and biases create a culture among policy makers that affects their decisions. These include confirmation bias (interpreting evidence in line with a pre-conceived idea), group reinforcement or 'group-think' (going along with a majority view even if an individual holds private doubts) and optimism bias (too great a view of one's own ability to make something happen in line with a plan). Confirmation bias has particularly significant implications for how we think about democratic politics and policy making, and is discussed in more detail in Chapters 7 and 11.

All policy actors making difficult decisions and implementing challenging plans will be subject to these kinds of biases to different degrees. How they play out in particular institutional contexts will be affected by the other elements of culture discussed above. For example norms around conformity and strong group identity may make the risk of group-think greater. Particular causal world-views will have a direct impact on how someone views different types of evidence, leading to different confirmation biases. The overall model of psychological shortcuts that we all use is often summarised as 'bounded rationality' (Simon, 1997): we are all rational, but only up to a point.

Culture and values in society

The discussion above has focused mainly on examples and evidence from the policy-making sphere. The culture of political and governmental institutions is indeed critical to policy outcomes, as will be made clear in the following chapters. However, this direct impact of culture and values on the policy-making process is only half of the story. The other element is the way in which culture produces social outcomes directly, without a public policy element. Policy makers then need to grapple with these outcomes and their constant re-invention as cultures evolve.

The work of anthropologist Clifford Geertz (1973) gives a widely-used approach to understanding the centrality of culture in explaining social actions and outcomes. He argues that culture is the 'fabric of meaning' that guides human action. That fabric of meaning cannot be found by looking at numerical data. Instead, social outcomes can only be explained and understood if we turn our attention to stories and symbols, rituals and cultures. In one of his most famous pieces of such understanding, Geertz immersed himself in the tradition of cockfighting in Bali. He found that the villagers would wager huge sums of money on these fights, to an extent that was irrational from any economic point of view. He explained these choices by pointing to a wider set of values and meaning around esteem, honour and dignity. The rituals around the cockfight did not just represent the Balinese culture but were central to creating it.

Geertz did not discover all this by reading a rule book about Balinese cockfighting, but by deep observation of how culture created outcomes. Reading a rule book is, in fact, very unlikely to ever give anyone a proper understanding of culture. Almost by definition, if what we are addressing is a thick fabric or web of social meaning that operates at many levels and through symbols and rituals, then anything written down is unlikely to do it justice. So throughout this book we will assume that the culture and values we are discussing are generally unwritten and implicit. Actors in the policy process need to infer them from seeing how people and institutions actually behave rather than from formal descriptions. There is some evidence that looking beyond written material and into deeper observation helps to understand policy processes. For example, in their study of economic policy making in Japan, Katayama and Ursprung (2004) showed that looking at what they call 'cultural idiosyncrasies' rather than written models was a much more effective way of explaining what actually happened.

Focusing on unwritten rules and behaviour creates a challenge. It means that it is unlikely to be clear which of the elements of culture and values is in play at any one time. Therefore we risk an analytical mush, where all of the different phenomena discussed so far in this chapter merge together. When going through the ways in which culture and values affect public policy, and the possible responses for policy makers, are we going to be clear what we are tackling at any given point?

The reality, however, is that all these elements do overlap and affect one another. Geertz's work shows vividly how many different levels interact to create the overall fabric of cultural meaning in a society. When each of us makes decisions every day, we do not stop to think whether we are being driven by behavioural psychological biases, or our moral opinions or social expectations and trust. Even if we did try to disentangle these factors there is no reason to suppose that we would be able to do so and in fact that very process of disentanglement would itself be just another process subject to all the same forces. Identifying different elements of culture and values would be even harder when observing a process second-hand. Therefore it will be necessary to keep culture and values as a multi-faceted concept. Different elements will be highlighted at different points in the argument in the following chapters, but they can never be entirely isolated from one another.

What we say or what we do?

The discussion above has focused on how culture and values come through in how people and institutions behave. It would make studying these phenomena much easier if there was a clear link between what people say about their culture and values and what they do. Studying Balinese cockfights as Geertz did must have been fascinating, but it required an extraordinary investment of time that is not often available. Is it possible to obtain useful information about culture and values in a simpler way, in particular by asking people directly?

There have been many attempts to do just that. One of the most famous and longstanding is the World Values Survey. This is an international collaboration across the social sciences, carrying out representative surveys in 100 countries covering almost 90 per cent of the world's population and addressing fundamental beliefs about morality and how the world works. The survey has been running since 1981, making it possible to look at change in values over time and how that interacts with what happens in different societies.

The World Values Survey, and other datasets of this type, are valuable for looking at macro-level differences in a way that detailed anthropological studies will simply never be able to match. Several of the studies and examples discussed in later chapters draw on this type of research. However, it is important to treat values surveys with a degree of caution. This is because people may say one thing to a survey agent but act entirely differently. Real values may be demonstrated by what people do, rather than what they say.

The difference between the two is particularly likely if the survey question touches on an issue where respondents feel there is a socially acceptable or expected answer. They could feel pressure to respond in a certain way, but do not actually behave in a manner consistent with their response. Values about the environment provide a good example of this. People may feel that they 'ought' to express a desire to preserve the environment. But when faced with having to live that value, potentially by imposing a cost or inconvenience on themselves, the reality may be rather different. Thapa (1999) conducted a study that showed precisely this outcome. He asked undergraduate students about their attitudes to the environment, measured on a standard scale, and found high levels of support for pro-environmental values. However, he then explored whether those same students actually carried out any of 24 environmental behaviours, for example reducing their car use, avoiding purchasing from companies with poor environmental records and seeking out biodegradable products. He found that, despite what the attitude survey had implied, most students did very little for the environment with the exception of recycling waste (probably the easiest option). Thapa also looked at the direct relationship between attitudes and behaviour. Were the students who were most environmental in their attitudes the most likely to behave accordingly? There was some relationship between the two, but Thapa concludes that it was 'weak or modest at best' (1999: 436). Therefore students who say they are the most environmental were not necessarily behaving in that way. This is hardly a ringing endorsement for the view that people will generally act in accordance with their stated values.

Conclusions like those from Thapa's work do not mean we should entirely write off what people say in surveys about values. The argument about socially acceptable answers in surveys won't apply to some questions, and is in any case context dependent. Many studies using the World Values Survey or similar datasets have found them to have considerable explanatory power, and some will be considered in later chapters. It is just important to remember the potential tension between what people say and what they do. Where there is a clear choice between the two, policy makers who care about impact in the real world would be well advised to lean towards the latter.

Conclusion

This chapter has introduced the concepts of culture and values and how they will be used in this book. They are inevitably overlapping and messy, with several elements in play at any time. Culture and values are important when looking at how policy makers themselves behave, and also for looking at how those policy makers and their decisions interact with society as a whole. The following chapters look at how all these elements come together to affect public policy and why policy makers need to take them seriously.

A final point is to note that I do not use 'culture' in this book as referring to the cultural sector of the economy (art, theatre, music and so on). As is hopefully clear by now I am taking 'culture' to be a much wider term (although there is interesting evidence on the strong political and policy preferences associated with people who work in those specific sectors).[2]

PART ONE

Why culture and values matter for public policy

Part One establishes the basic premise for the argument in the rest of the book. This is that culture and values have a significant role to play in determining how the policy process works and what its outcomes are. Each chapter in this Part sets out a different reason for adopting this premise.

2

Culture determines
whether policies work

History tells us that some policy challenges are intractable. I saw evidence of this first hand when I was the junior civil servant in the Cabinet Office team responsible for writing the Queen's Speech. This is the formal address that the British monarch gives at the start of every session of Parliament, setting out the government's forthcoming programme of legislation. The Speech is a grand ceremonial occasion, full of historical symbolism. The words themselves are printed on special 'goatskin' paper[1] and handed to the Sovereign in a velvet bag. Being part of the Speech process showed me that not only did the ceremony hardly change over time, but the policy challenges governments faced also stayed remarkably constant.

I saw this continuity because I was asked to go back over many Speeches from past years in order to get a feel for the language used and to see if there were lessons for those given on occasions similar to that I was working on (in this case a Speech immediately after a general election). What immediately struck me, after summoning many past texts from the depths of the Cabinet Office archives, was how for more than 50 years governments had been promising roughly the same things, often in near-identical words. All these administrations were going to improve health services, raise standards in schools and lower unemployment. Legislation would be needed to address crime and protect the environment. The challenges never seemed to go away, but to recur in similar forms for every generation of political leaders.

The governments who had produced these Speeches had tried lots of different policy tools. Some had favoured market incentives and the outsourcing of public services. Others had preferred high spending in the state sector. Some had wanted to devolve more to local government, others to centralise more control. Over the years, civil servants preparing policy advice for ministers, politicians advancing programmes for government, journalists commenting on policy issues and academics analysing the results all looked at the merits of these different tools. The same policy challenges seemed to persist, despite whatever governments of all political persuasions had thrown at them.

This chapter argues that culture and values are an important factor in understanding the ineffectiveness of many of the policies announced in all those Queen's Speeches over many years, by explaining how they help to determine policy outcomes. The first part of the chapter establishes theoretical reasons for believing that policy outcomes are dependent on culture to a significant degree. The second part then looks at some evidence to support the theoretical claim, drawn from research around the world.

The theory of why culture matters

I have held many roles in which 'strategy' has been part of my job title. When learning about strategy work, and subsequently teaching it to others myself, a famous quote usually attributed to the management guru Peter Drucker has always been front and centre. He (allegedly) said 'Culture eats strategy for breakfast'.[2] The essential point being made in the quote is that a strategy can look great on paper, coherent and compelling, but is entirely useless if everyone in the organisation it is being applied to behaves in ways that undermine it. I believe that the experience of governments in attempting to resolve policy problems over the years demonstrates that after consuming strategy for breakfast, culture goes on to consume policy tools of all types for lunch. Policy, like strategy, has little impact, or certainly not the intended impact, if it is contrary to the culture of the organisation that has to implement it. Why is this?

One of the most compelling theoretical arguments for why culture trumps policy design comes from the work of Michael Lipsky (1979). He argued that the reality of policy outcomes emerges from the actions of front-line public service workers, or in his famous phrase 'street-level bureaucrats'. In his view, policy outcomes are driven by how a teacher interacts with a class, which person a police officer chooses to arrest, which potential patient receives more attention from the community nurse. Thousands of individual decisions about the delivery of public services are being made every day, each one creating a small policy consequence. The front-line workers are often under pressure, with limited resources and demands from the public that they cannot meet. They also have all the normal human pressures faced by any employee, like caring responsibilities at home or irritating colleagues. Lipsky argues that the workers adopt coping strategies to mitigate these pressures, such as prioritising which instructions to follow, where to focus their time and where shortcuts can be made. These strategies necessarily emerge from their existing worldviews and the unwritten rules and practices (or culture) of the delivery organisations they work in. Seen in this context, a central policy initiative is just one pressure among the many that need to be coped with. It too is filtered through the habits and cultures that the relevant workers have evolved.

Central government policy makers are, of course, aware that front-line workers may ignore, distort or shortcut new initiatives. They have some strategies of their own to try to ensure that those new directions are taken more seriously. One such strategy is to set a target for performance and mandate front-line delivery agencies to report regularly on whether they are hitting it. Failure to do so leads to some form of sanction for the senior managers responsible. A well-known example of a target approach in the United Kingdom was the introduction of a four-hour limit for time patients would have to wait at hospital accident and emergency units before being treated. Such a target looks feasible when there is a very specific service standard that the policy maker is focused on. A different situation is where the policy maker is more interested in the performance of a whole institution against a set of different objectives, rather than a single service metric. In this case a common approach is to create an inspection regime. Someone accountable to and employed by the centre spends time in the delivery institution to ensure that it is operating in the way that the centre intends. An example of this is the Ofsted inspection system for schools in England and Wales. A team of inspectors visits each school and makes an overall judgement on its performance against a set of criteria developed at the centre, which is then published in an attempt to ensure accountability.

Experience demonstrates, however, that both of these enforcement strategies are weak. There are two reasons for this. First, both of them struggle to cope when confronted with the reality of large dispersed policy delivery systems. There are so many street-level bureaucrats interacting in so many complex ways that no target can cover everything and no inspector can understand the constantly changing interactions. As Hayek (1944) famously argued in the context of economic planning, once society reaches a certain level of modern complexity it is simply impossible for central institutions to monitor what is going on and understand how different actors relate to one another in a dynamic environment.

The second reason that both of the control mechanisms often fail is that central controls are seen by the front-line staff as just another thing to cope with, like any other central instruction. Local organisational cultures and habits enable ways to deal with the controls and subvert their original purpose, as with any other policy input. We can see this with the experience of the four-hour emergency unit waiting target mentioned above. Providing sufficient resources and re-designing processes to hit this target in hospitals facing other significant pressures was very difficult. It became clear that some hospitals found it easier to meet the letter of the target than the spirit. The four-hour countdown measured by the target started once a patient entered the emergency unit. Therefore in some cases managers decided that the way to meet the target (on paper at least) was to leave patients outside in an ambulance rather than have them enter the unit at all (Ken et al, 2010). This approach made their performance against the target look more acceptable, while certainly not improving the service received by the public.

Inspection regimes face similar challenges. The phrase 'Potemkin Village' originates in the (probably apocryphal) story about fake villages built to impress Catherine the Great when she inspected parts of the Russian Empire. Modern public sector inspectorates worry about similar deception on a more mundane level. I once accompanied the Inspector of Prisons and his team on a visit to a large prison in one of England's major cities. Prison Inspectorate policy was to give little warning of the visit, so that there was no opportunity to create unrepresentative positive conditions. Even with this precaution the inspection team were always aware that staff and inmates would behave differently when they were around and would not necessarily be candid about the true situation. An inspection is only ever temporary and cannot change the underlying cultures and expectations.

As a result of the challenges of central control, John (1998) argues that the street level is so important that the decisions taken there during implementation are as important as those taken by 'policy makers' in the classic sense, and that those front-line decisions are heavily shaped by the culture of the institutions that are in place. Taken to its logical conclusion, this line of argument points to a view that policy is not 'made' at all. It emerges from 'self-organising networks' (Rhodes, 1997) of interactions between all the different players in what is often a complex system. The phrase 'self-organising' points to the importance of habits, assumptions and unwritten rules – one of the forms of culture identified in Chapter 1 – in this policy formation process.

Evidence of why culture matters

The theoretical case for the importance of culture that comes out in Lipsky and other work is borne out by evidence and experience. I experienced the power of culture at the street level to frustrate central policy edicts and shape important outcomes when I was a board member at a Primary Care Trust in West London. Primary Care Trusts (which no longer exist) were at that time responsible for overseeing all the general practice doctors in our patch. The central National Health Service (NHS) often issued targets and new priorities that the general practices were expected to meet. The staff in my Trust were very focused on these: their future NHS careers were heavily dependent on showing good performance to the management layer above (who covered the whole of London and would compare them against others elsewhere in the city). I chaired what was called the Performance Monitoring Committee, which four times a year would go through how we were doing against all the targets.

What became clear from that review process was that there was huge variation in performance against the targets between the different doctors' practices across the area. In particular we seemed to have some that were repeatedly weaker against all of the things we were measuring. They persuaded fewer people to join programmes that would help them stop smoking. They prescribed more of the drugs that were no longer recommended as the best clinical response to the relevant conditions. The differential performance extended to administrative issues as well as clinical ones, such as completing entries on databases or recording which checks had been carried out on which patients. All of the practices faced the same policy framework and the same incentives (financial and managerial) to perform. So why did those levers appear to work in some cases but not others?

The area my Trust was responsible for had typical Inner London extremes: some of the wealthiest streets in Europe not far from estates among the most deprived in the country. So we looked to see if demographics explained the different performance. Maybe some practices were just struggling because of the pressures in the communities in which they operated? On deeper inspection we couldn't find such a link. There were doctors in some of the deprived areas delivering an excellent service and responding to new policy initiatives with alacrity.

After digging through the data one factor emerged that linked the practices that were not performing against the targets. This was the length of time that the doctors had been operating. Those scoring lower had overwhelmingly been in business for a long time, and their practices had not taken on many new clinicians. It should perhaps not have been surprising that longstanding doctors were more resistant to change, less willing to jump to what might have seemed like an arbitrary new priority from the national leadership. These practices had developed a culture of doing things in a certain way. They had presumably also realised that given all the burdens on local NHS management there was a limit to how hard and how consistently they would be pushed to change. So their patients experienced the outcomes of health policy very differently to their neighbours just across the road in the catchment area of another practice. That difference was down to the culture of the practice and the approach of the front-line staff.

The scale of the difference in outcome is important here. The gaps between even the median practice (not the top performers) and the lowest were huge on some of the targets, 50 per cent or more. It is unlikely that a policy change at the level of the whole system, for example a plausible funding increase or decrease, could ever shift an outcome by 50 per cent. Culture really was eating policy for lunch in this case. The reluctance of longstanding doctors to shift their habits and or listen to new NHS directives was more important to what happened than any policy tweaks at the centre.

This example addresses culture at a local level and how differences of culture between front-line workers really matters. The importance of culture in determining policy outcomes also emerges strongly if we look at a larger scale, whole countries or regions within countries. There is a lot of evidence that macro policy outcomes are very heavily influenced by culture, and cultural difference means that policy frameworks implemented in one place come out very differently elsewhere.

The strongest evidence for this point comes from international development studies. Anyone who works in the development field will have experienced the phenomenon of a set of rules or policies that made perfect sense, often in the context of a developed OECD country, failing entirely or even creating a negative outcome once an aid programme has paid for its introduction to a different context. A World Bank review of programmes to improve governance in developing countries demonstrated the challenges of importing models from elsewhere and found they often failed (World Bank, 2008b). The Institute of Development Studies (2010) conducted a five-year-long study into this phenomenon, looking at development programmes across the world. They concluded that informal institutions and relationships were essential to understanding development. In their view, it is misguided to see interventions to create new policies and rule-based systems as the best way to promote development. Instead, they argue that we need 'to start not with improving delivery mechanisms, but with a much better understanding of the local social, institutional and political dynamics' (Institute of Development Studies, 2010: 76). Effective state authority and governance are critical to help the development process, and the report argues that 'informal institutions and ... relationships' (Institute of Development Studies, 2010: 7) are where we should look for the ways in to improving them.

Some of the specific examples drawn out in the report illustrate powerfully the relative importance of culture to driving outcomes. Patunru et al (2009) studied the economies of two cities in Indonesia, with a particular focus on their success in attracting investment. The cities had similar populations and similar size economies. However, they had very different policy environments. One had an economic development plan that had been developed in an inclusive way by the local government and different economic and social groups, while the other did not. The city with the good plan also enjoyed a good system of regulation: it had established a new streamlined licensing system and local business perceptions of the regulatory regime were positive. In contrast, in the other city, over 80 per cent of small- and medium-sized enterprises (SMEs) thought the licensing process was corrupt.

If policy was critical to driving outcomes, we would expect the city with a good plan and effective regulation to enjoy higher levels of investment and economic growth. In fact, there was virtually no difference between the two. Growth was strong for both, including in the plan-less and corrupt environment. The research team conducted in-depth interviews to get behind this confusing picture. They discovered that in the city with what looked like weaker policies, a culture of cooperation and close relationships, largely outside the formal government system, enabled decisions to be taken that supported high levels of business investment. Looking just at the policy, without these deeper cultural factors, would have been entirely misleading.

Two Indonesian cities provide an interesting case study, but there is also compelling evidence from the two largest geopolitical transitions in recent times: the collapse of the Soviet Union and the economic rise of China. In the Soviet case, the full armoury of policy tools was deployed in the early 1990s in an attempt to help Russia and the other Soviet successor republics make a transition to a liberal capitalist economic and political model. Murrell (1993: 114) describes that armoury as:

> fiscal and monetary austerity, a convertible currency, deregulation of prices, de-monopolisation of the state sector, the removal of barriers to international trade ... the creation of new rules for international trade, tax reform, unemployment insurance and job training schemes credit allocation to small businesses and privatisation.

This dramatic and comprehensive approach was to run aground on the rocks of culture.

I received a first-hand impression of quite how different the post-Soviet culture remained when compared to Western Europe when I was in charge of the UK government's bilateral aid programme to Ukraine and Russia, from 2003 to 2005. Fifteen years after the start of transition and those dramatic policy changes outlined above, the reality remained a long way from the reformers' aspirations. I have a vivid memory of a meeting in a small provincial Ukrainian city where we were funding a programme of reform in the regional government. As the important visitor from London I was brought in to meet all the senior officials from the local administration. The meeting took place in a massive conference room, one wall of which was entirely given over to a map of the USSR with its pre-1990 borders. After a very stilted formal meeting I asked a Ukrainian member of my team if she had been able to see what was written on the piece of paper that one of the senior officials had stared at for the entire time. She replied cheerily that it was the report from the security services on everyone who was attending the meeting. It is perhaps not surprising that, with such different codes of behaviour and continued attachment to the practices and symbols of Soviet power, policies came out with rather different results from what we intended.

This is just an anecdote, but there is also considerable academic research that demonstrates how culture in the post-Soviet space consumed the policy tools of the Western reformers. Yakovlev (2006) and Hanson and Teague (2005) show that introducing the tools listed above into a culture of centralised power and deference to the personal authority of a superior in the hierarchy meant they operated differently from the way anticipated. Instead of creating a decentralised system of competition with capital and labour being efficiently allocated, the prevailing culture meant that new tools of regulation and corporate ownership were used by well-connected political insiders to accumulate personal wealth and the expense of the state and then to eliminate potential sources of competition for both money and power.

The Soviet example shows patronage, connections and closed networks being used to frustrate change and to hamper attempts to spread wealth and opportunity more broadly. The Chinese experience is almost the opposite. If policy tools were the reason for China's economic success, we would have expected to see the rapid period of growth preceded by the introduction of some of the classic tools associated with economic innovation, for example reforms that safeguard property rights and promote the rule of law. However digging into the Chinese growth story demonstrates nothing of the sort. Qian (2003) found that informal relationships and close local networks of cooperation that were enabled by the culture and common values of the Communist party cadres were, at least in the early stages, effectively taking the place of formal property rights. Members of these groups trusted one another to respect certain boundaries despite the lack of a policy framework. Another study (Hampton, 2006) compared the performance of the economic development agencies in two different Chinese cities. While the policy under which both operated was the same, one was much more effective. The study concluded that this was because there were stronger informal personal relationships between senior officials in the successful city, which gave them access to different ways of solving problems. So once again, informal connections and ways of doing business drive outcomes in a stronger way than policy.

Conclusion

This chapter set out to demonstrate that culture and values are important because they shape policy outcomes. Governments often struggle to make progress on complex social problems, with repeated policy initiatives leaving intractable challenges in place. There is a strong theoretical case for arguing that this is at least in part due to the fact that implementation is carried out by dispersed front-line staff, who interpret and adapt policy imperatives according to their own values and assumptions and those of the organisations they work in. This theoretical case is supported by extensive evidence. At a micro level, differences in culture seem to explain considerable amounts of the variation in performance between individual public service delivery organisations, and different localities operating within the same national policy. It also helps to explain some outcomes at a national level. The impact of culture can be both positive and negative. The Soviet experience gives an example of where policy with positive intent was thwarted by cultural factors, whereas China could be seen as an example of where economic transformation occurred in the absence of many policies that were thought to be important, because cultural norms acted as a substitute. This direct link between culture and policy outcomes is the most obvious reason that policy makers need to care about culture and values. The following three chapters set out some others which I believe are equally important.

3

Culture and values determine whether policies are legitimate

This chapter explores another reason why culture and values matter to policy makers, namely legitimacy. Many policies rely on their being accepted by citizens as legitimate in order to work. At one level, this is really just another version of the argument in the previous chapter that culture affects outcomes: as the first part of this chapter shows, a failure of legitimacy means the policy will not achieve what it was intended to. The second part takes the case further, demonstrating that legitimacy is important in and of itself, regardless of its effect on whether a policy works. What counts as legitimacy is heavily dependent on culture and values. Therefore it is not possible to ensure that a policy is legitimate unless we take those factors into account.

First, it is important to define what 'legitimacy' means. In political science it is generally held to be the situation where a state authority and its actions have power because of consent and mutual understanding rather than coercion. Using a simple example, a legitimate tax is one that people pay on time and without pressure. An illegitimate one needs to be collected by sending revenue service officers or the police to force payment. Legitimacy is a subjective concept, dependent on the beliefs held by the citizens (Weber, 1978). Therefore what counts as legitimate varies according to context, which is a point we will return to later in the chapter when looking at how culture and values affect what counts as 'legitimate'.

Legitimacy is needed to deliver policy

One of the events that made the greatest impression on me when I was starting to get interested in politics and policy was the poll tax riot in London in the spring of 1990. I had never seen mass street violence in England on the news before. I remember asking my parents why people were rioting and what this 'poll tax' was. They explained to me that people were rioting because they thought the new tax was unfair, and the government wasn't listening to them. The idea that a policy needed to be fair, and people needed to agree that it was fair, stuck with me.

The poll tax experience is an excellent example of what can happen if a policy isn't regarded as legitimate and breaches the boundaries of what is socially acceptable. Adonis et al (1994) produced the definitive account of the poll tax experience. I personally think that it should be required reading for anyone working in the British government, for its compelling account of how seemingly sensible people and established institutions could throw up such a disastrous policy. Their work shows that the rioters I asked my parents about were not the only people who held similar views about the new policy. By 1990 only 25 per cent of the population considered that the poll tax was fair (Adonis et al, 1994: 260). This was a very low level for a policy that could not survive long if people refused to cooperate with it. In the section of their book entitled 'Why Did it Fail?' Adonis et al (1994: 289) say 'First, it proved impossible to collect a large portion of the tax in many … areas, where mobility, hostility and tacit evasion defeated the administrative resources of local authorities'. The argument is that a lack of consent and mutual understanding (from our definition of legitimacy above) ultimately proved fatal for the government's flagship policy.

Legitimacy is as important for routine day-to-day functions of government as it is for major reforms like the poll tax. This point comes into sharp relief in policing, as in the commonly used phrase 'policing by consent'. The way in which the police use powers to stop and search citizens on the street is a particularly pointed example of how consent works alongside state power.

This power held by the police is the way in which the coercive capacity of the state comes into closest and most regular contact with large numbers of citizens. That power has long been a controversial one, especially regarding whether some police forces stop and search members of certain ethnic groups in disproportionate way. Bradford (2017) conducted an in-depth analysis of the use of stop and search by police forces in the United Kingdom. He found that the power could, if misused, undermine public trust and confidence in the police more generally. This occurred particularly if police forces prioritised carrying out large volumes of searches rather than focusing on where those actions might be most effective in tackling crime, what Bradford calls a quantity rather than a quality strategy. He argues that this loss of trust and confidence makes policing as a whole less effective and undermines the legitimacy of the state overall.

In a less dramatic example, also from the criminal justice sphere, I was involved in developing the policy framework to underpin a major programme of reform to the court system in England and Wales. These reforms were intended to speed up justice as well as reducing costs, all facilitated by technology. We explored whether some very low-level matters (such as penalties for some traffic offences or prosecuting fare evasion on public transport) could be dealt with outside the physical courts entirely, using digital means. There seemed to be potential to save time and complexity for everyone concerned, freeing up trained staff and legal personnel to focus on more serious matters. However, we were very much aware that we were wrestling not just with an IT programme but with fundamental questions about legitimacy. Would the public regard an online process as fair, to the same extent as they had done for hundreds of years when the events took place in a courtroom? Would it be possible to create the right safeguards, for example for people who might find using some digital channels difficult? External pressure groups were, understandably, concerned about all these issues and determined to keep pressure on us at the Ministry of Justice.[1] We knew that if the new system did not seem legitimate people would not engage with it, would seek to evade justice or potentially challenge decisions in higher courts. All of these outcomes would fundamentally undermine our policy objectives of reduced cost and efficiency, and so legitimacy was key. At the time of writing, debates about what level of digitisation would be acceptable in the court system are still continuing.

The intrinsic value of legitimacy

The poll tax, stop and search, and online courts are all examples of policies that cannot meet their objectives unless they are felt to be legitimate. There is, however, a deeper point around legitimacy. Legitimacy has a value in itself, regardless of whether that helps the policy meet its goals. This intrinsic value becomes clear when we consider what people want from and value in the policy process. One way to demonstrate the intrinsic value of legitimacy is to use a simple thought experiment. Imagine a small town with farmland around it. A proposal is made to build some new houses on part of that land. The town has already held a series of public consultations about a local planning framework, which sets out criteria for the kinds of situations in which development will be allowed on farmland. The framework also specifies the design and the affordability of housing that will be given priority. When the farmer and developer make their proposal about this particular piece of land there is an inquiry, chaired by someone independent from outside the locality, which explores whether this new proposal meets the criteria in the plan. After agreeing some modifications to the proposed development to address points raised in the inquiry, the developer receives permission from the local council to go ahead. Some local people are not happy at the loss of countryside, but accept that they had the opportunity to have their say and that the process was reasonable.

Contrast this example with a different version of the same scenario. This time there is no local plan agreeing principles for when and what housing should be built. The developer submits their proposal to the local council, and for many weeks nothing happens. There is no information about how the decision will be made or under what criteria. Then late on a Friday evening at the start of a holiday period a small notice appears on the council website saying that permission has been granted for the development to proceed, and construction on the land starts within days. The outcome is exactly the same (let us assume for the sake of argument that in the second version the council has insisted in private on all the adjustments to the development proposal that emerged from the public process in the first version). The same houses are built on the same land in the same way. However, it is clear that there is something inherently valuable about the first process in contrast to the second. If you asked people which scenario they would prefer to live through, you would expect a strong majority for the first. This implies that a fair, open and legitimate process is valuable to people regardless of whether or not it affects the real-world outcome.

The view that legitimacy and trust in the process is something that people value and therefore is something that policy makers should aim for has been explored in extensive research on the theme of 'public value'. This area of work attempts to take a broad view of what the goals of public policy ought to be, drawing in concepts like legitimacy. In a report that I was involved in at the UK Cabinet Office (Kelly et al, 2002), we argued that there are three broad categories of public value. These are services (what citizens receive directly from the state, such as treatment in hospital), outcomes (which may result from services but also wider policies, such as good health) and trust/legitimacy (services and outcomes operating in a fair way, such as the health system prioritising patients according to sensible and transparent criteria).

There is good evidence from public opinion surveys that people do value fairness and legitimacy independently of how they consume services and outcomes provided by the state. Looking at how people relate to public services, one study found that 66 per cent of people referred to their relationship with public services as being that of 'citizens or members of the public' compared to only 30 per cent who thought of themselves as 'customers or users' (Public Management Foundation, 1996). The favoured terminology implies an interest in the services delivered to other people in a way that is not the case with most private sector services. The same study found that 79 per cent of people agreed with the statement that 'public services should be targeted at those with greatest need'. Crucially, this percentage hardly varied at all between socioeconomic groups. Therefore it cannot be explained by people believing that they should benefit personally from the distributional choices. Instead, it seems most plausible to interpret it as a broader desire for a form of fairness at the level of society as a whole. Another study showed that whether people used privately funded alternatives to public services had very little impact on their propensity to support higher levels of state spending on those services (Institute for Fiscal Studies, 1997). Again this implies that people value some form of fairness in the way policy is targeted, regardless of whether or not that benefits them or their families directly.

This model of public value with three elements has also been endorsed by more recent work. Pulling together insights from years of work in government innovation and improvement, Nesta (2019a) came up with essentially the same elements: services, outcomes and justice. They note the importance of 'integrity, reliability and responsiveness' (Nesta, 2019a: 10) of the government alongside more tangible outcomes. They also point to a positive feedback loop between trust in governing institutions and trust between citizens. A government that acts in a trustworthy and legitimate way therefore creates benefits independently of the services it is providing, given that trust between citizens is a valuable public good, as shown in Chapter 1. A variant on this argument about how acting in a legitimate way creates benefits comes from the 'Finding Legitimacy' programme run by the Centre for Public Impact. It argues that legitimacy is essential to making governments and societies resilient to future challenges (Centre for Public Impact, 2018). It may be possible for governments to operate for some time with low levels of legitimacy. But when societies need to adapt to shocks and innovate, governments need to start doing new things. A lack of legitimacy means that these innovations are less likely to be accepted, giving public authorities less margin for error. So there is a value to legitimacy over and above its impact on services and outcomes at any one time. That value lies in the solid bedrock it creates on which to build the responses to new challenges.

Why culture and values determine what is legitimate

At this point we need to bring the discussion back to culture and values. If we agree legitimacy is important, why does that entail a focus on culture and values by policy makers? The reason relates to a point made at the start of this chapter: legitimacy is a subjective concept. What counts as legitimate depends on the context. The context-specific nature of legitimacy is very clear from Max Weber's formulation referred to above. Weber (1978) identifies three types of legitimacy. The first is traditional legitimacy, derived from custom and continuity, the government's role being accepted because that is the way things have always been. Traditional tribal societies and monarchies have strong elements of this type of legitimacy. The second is charismatic legitimacy, derived from the personal authority of a particular leader. Governing institutions are less important in this type, which is often associated with autocracy or theocracy. The third is rational–legal legitimacy, where state institutions establish a system of law that is accepted by the population. The examples discussed so far in this chapter, coming as they do from contemporary liberal democracies, are more of this type.

These context differences that create different forms of legitimacy are intimately associated with culture. If we go back to the definitions of culture discussed in Chapter 1, and particularly Geertz's work, we can see that the three types of legitimacy have different cultural bases. Geertz emphasised the importance of stories, symbols and rituals as foundations of culture. Those stories, symbols and rituals have very different manifestations in societies with Weber's three forms of legitimacy. These different rituals are important to reinforcing the acceptance of the different forms of authority that carry legitimacy in those societies.

Starting with societies that rest on traditional legitimacy, they face their greatest challenge at points of transition: how can it be made clear that the new ruler is a true heir of the history from which they derive their authority? A sense of custom and continuity is needed, and for this reason traditional legitimacy societies often have elaborate ceremonies that are repeated almost exactly from one transition of power to another. Ancien Regime France provides an excellent example. All French kings from 1027 onwards were crowned at Rheims. The final prerevolution monarch, Louis XVI, deployed a hugely elaborate traditional ceremony with costly regalia in an attempt to reinforce his traditional authority, despite the near-bankruptcy facing the French state at this time. One contemporary witness said the whole spectacle was so successful (at least in the short term) that 'spontaneous tears of joy ran down every cheek' (Baker, 1978: 279).

In contrast, charismatic legitimacy depends on ceremonies that reinforce the position of an individual leader, as someone unique and potentially as a break from history rather than part of it. Hitler's Nuremburg rallies are a famous and extreme example of this very different type of symbolism. Rational-legal societies also have rituals and ceremonies that reinforce the cultural assumptions on which their legitimacy rests, and they can still have an element of drama, if not quite on the scale of a 16th-century French coronation. The inauguration of a President of the United States certainly demonstrates this: an oath of office which stresses defence of the constitution, administered before an assembled mass of citizens by the most senior member of the judiciary. The whole set-up emphasises the twin values of the rule of law and public consent on which a modern liberal rational-legal society rests.

These ceremonies draw a clear line between culture and legitimacy. Values come more strongly into play when we consider fairness. It is clear from the discussion above on the poll tax and other examples that fairness is a central part of legitimacy. People are more likely to think a policy, or a whole way of governing, is legitimate if it accords with their view of fairness. Fairness is rooted strongly in ethical values and it is not possible to discuss what is fair without framing the conversation in those terms. Is fairness equality of outcome or equality of opportunity? Or to put it in terms more often used by ethicists, are we interested in consequentialist fairness (what happens) or principles of fair conduct (how we get there)? These choices are often the starting point of moral philosophy courses, at least in the United Kingdom and the United States.[2]

To take the concept of fairness out of philosophy lectures and into something of more practical use to policy makers, we can look at the legal system. This is where a modern rational-legitimate society expresses, in practical procedural terms, what fairness looks like. In the British context at least, fairness and legitimacy are explicitly tied together in the legal framework for looking at whether government or other public bodies are operating in an appropriate way. When I was a new graduate joining the British civil service, my cohort of recruits was sent on a training course with the rather threatening title 'The Judge Over Your Shoulder'. It was all about the legal framework for government decision making and what we should or shouldn't do to avoid ending up on the wrong end of a court judgement. The most important concept, which has stuck with me throughout my policy making career, is of 'legitimate expectations'. This is, in summary, the idea that the government creates by past actions and statements an expectation that people will be treated in a certain way, and that way is accepted on all sides as fair and reasonable. The expectation has a form of legitimacy, grounded in that acquiescence that it is fair and reflects a set of values about how people should be treated. If governments cut across these legitimate expectations (most often by failing to consult people properly on something that affects them) then a judge may require a policy to be paused for reflection and change. This whole area of practice is an incarnation, in precise practical steps, of social values about what is fair, and therefore legitimate.

Conclusion

It is clear that policy making has to take account of legitimacy. Without it many policies will simply not work. In addition, regardless of whether they work or not, illegitimate policies are intrinsically less valuable to individual citizens or society as a whole. People value legitimacy even if it has no effect on outcomes. Legitimate action by government also creates the positive spin-offs of greater social trust more generally and more resilience to future shocks. Legitimacy rests on context and is both expressed in cultural symbols and intimately bound up with notions of fairness. Therefore only an understanding of culture (and its relationship to symbols) and values (which determine concepts of fairness) enables a policy maker to understand and work with legitimacy in the way necessary to success.

4

Arguments about values and the purpose of democracy

This chapter considers a different reason for putting culture and values at the heart of policy making. It moves away from the issues of whether policies work or not, and whether people accept them. Instead, it focuses on looking more deeply at the purpose of politics in a democratic society, and the central place that values have in determining that.

Values determine the realm of politics

Why are some questions political and others not? Open a newspaper or log on to a news website and there will be a section called 'politics' which covers what is going on in political institutions: the latest news from an election campaign or what is being debated in Congress or Parliament. Then in other sections there will be coverage of events that still have a strong political component: perhaps whether a new medical treatment will be publicly funded, or a report on endangered wildlife that leads to debate on the effectiveness of policies for environmental protection. There will then also be a whole set of stories with no political content at all, about interesting happenings in entertainment, sport and everyday lives.

It seems obvious and natural that politics comes into some spheres and not others. But what counts as 'political' doesn't stay the same. It differs over time and between countries. To illustrate how the content of political debate changes, I looked at Hansard to see what the British House of Commons was debating exactly 150 years to the day before I was writing the first draft of this chapter. On 13 July 1868 the main issue before the House was the Royal Navy. The Navy's overall budget or strategy would still be seen as important political issues today, but this debate had a very different focus. Members of Parliament were discussing, in an extraordinary level of detail, the design and performance of different types of ship. One Member, Captain MacKinnon, was very concerned that 'main deck outside the battery' of one type of vessel 'was only plated with iron 5–16ths of an inch thick'. Others discussed the maximum speed of a new ship design in different wind conditions.[1] I imagine the engineers responsible for building hugely complex modern warships are grateful that the number of sixteenths of an inch involved in the armour plating is a matter for technical analysis by them rather than debate in the House of Commons. What counts as the proper matter for political debate has changed.

What feels 'political' in one country can feel strange to someone from elsewhere, even for countries at a similar stage of economic development and therefore facing similar challenges. For example, many Europeans are surprised by the central place that abortion law holds in US political debate, and that it is seen by some voters as a key test of whether a certain candidate is acceptable. How far the judicial process should be affected by politics is another question that varies widely between countries. Judges and or prosecutors are elected in some US states, and it is entirely normal to talk about a certain court having a Republican or Democrat majority. In Spain examining magistrates have become highly political figures, most famously Baltasar Garzon who pursued an inquiry into events under Franco's dictatorship that had previously been covered by an amnesty. In contrast to these models, in England and Wales judges and prosecutors are non-political figures, appointed through a process deliberately designed to preserve professional neutrality and to prevent their political views from becoming relevant or even known.

One of the key factors that determines whether or not an issue becomes political in a given context is whether there is a dispute about values at the heart of it. To demonstrate this, we can use a thought experiment about league tables. Every year the English football Premier League has a table which makes it clear which team is the champion, which teams get relegated to the lower Championship for the next season, and so on. Few issues inspire more passion for much of the population than the relative performance of their favoured football team. And yet anyone saying that the football league table had anything to do with politics would be seen as crazy.

Another form of league table that is common in England applies to schools. Schools in a given local area are ranked, in a process that generates huge interest. Estate agents advertise that the property they are selling is near a highly-rated school. Local councils have to conduct spot checks to make sure that people aren't applying for schools under false pretences, like using the address of a relative who lives nearer to one at the top of the league. While the level of excitement and interest may be similar to the football league tables, the schools example is highly political. Every year politicians, teachers unions and other commentators praise or denigrate the league tables, saying that they are measuring the right or wrong things, benefiting one group of schools or pupils unfairly while damaging another, putting too much pressure on teachers or students or creating powerful incentives and so on.[2]

So, what is the fundamental difference between football league tables and school league tables? It is that one of them requires value judgements and one does not. In the football case, the league table is measuring performance against an objectively agreed standard. Did your team win or draw enough games in the season to finish ahead of another team, or not? Winning and drawing are measured by a very simple thing (goals) that everyone can see and agree on. The only value judgement made in the construction of a football league table is that a win is worth three times as much as a draw.[3] Underlying all this is a total consensus on what constitutes a good result in football: scoring more goals than the opposition within the rules of the game.

There is no such consensus on what a 'good result' in education looks like. Therefore the league tables are measuring something entirely different, namely one interpretation of how to measure what good looks like. Different views on what is 'good' are pervasive in education. At the level of the system as a whole, is it better to improve average performance, or the performance of the most disadvantaged, or the performance of the most able? What choice you make is itself driven by deeper value judgements: is overall economic performance more important than how the benefits of economic growth are distributed? Is economic performance actually the purpose of education anyway?

Even if people manage to agree a common approach to the overall aim of the education system, they may hold very different values about what it is worthwhile to learn. When I was an undergraduate I went to a talk at a university society by the then Chief Inspector of Schools, Chris Woodhead. He was known for his traditional views about what school subjects were worthwhile, and made some scathing remarks about the value of media studies. As it happened, and rather unusually for someone at a highly academic university, I had done media studies as one of my A Levels. I believed that it had in many ways been more challenging than my other, much more 'traditional' subjects and told him so. I doubt the rather incoherent intervention of an annoyed undergraduate had any impact on Mr Woodhead's value judgement. But our disagreement around these values illustrated why school league tables are so likely to become a political issue.

I would be very surprised if I could have resolved my argument with the Chief Inspector of Schools by appealing to facts and evidence. Even if I had shown that, for example, there were lots of ex-media studies students like me who had gone on to do well at leading universities, he could have argued that this pointed to an admissions process prepared to overlook the fundamental worthlessness of what I had studied in favour of underlying potential. Or if he had demonstrated that people with media studies qualifications earned much lower salaries than their equivalents with other subjects, my undergraduate self would probably have responded that this showed that the economy was structurally unfair and valued the wrong things, rather than anything about the nature of media studies.

Trying to resolve arguments about values by appealing to facts feels pointless. The great Cambridge philosopher G E Moore termed this problem 'the naturalistic fallacy' or, to put it in simpler terms, the impossibility of deriving an 'ought' statement from an 'is' statement about empirical facts (Moore, 1903). Moore's point is that there is a fundamental difference between statements of fact and statements of value. There is a different decision, a different kind of thought, in moving from one to the other. How much money different people have is a fact. Whether or not that is unfair and should be addressed by political action is a value and there is no logical or inevitable link from one thought to the other.

Resolving values-based arguments

The football league table sits purely in the realm of facts, and disputes about it can be resolved through simply checking the scores and some basic maths. Resolving values-based disputes about issues like education is harder, and every society needs a way of doing so. Put very crudely, there are three choices.

The first is for someone, or some group, to simply decide. They are given (or take) the right to determine the 'ought' questions and if necessary to use state power to enforce that judgement. Decisions about what local output targets to set and how to measure them in the USSR's five-year plans were no less value-based than decisions on how to construct school league tables. But the Soviet system resolved any potential arguments by simply giving Stalin, or whoever ran the system at the time, the right to decide how things ought to be and to impose their values on everyone else. This option is only really open to states where legitimacy follows one of the first two of Weber's types as discussed in Chapter 3: traditional or charismatic.

The second is to keep value judgements private and away from the state, so it doesn't matter if people disagree. This is possible up to a point, and is part of the way modern democracies work. To give a simple example, I like modern abstract art but many people don't. If I buy some prints and display them in my house, or go to a suitable exhibition, that doesn't impose any costs on anyone who thinks that abstract art is rubbish. This disagreement about values therefore does not need any sort of public or political process and it is entirely possible for people to rub along together. (Of course the Soviet approach set out above considered this sort of private value judgement rather differently. In a totalitarian state there is no such thing as a private expression of a value judgement. Even hanging a picture where no-one else could see or listening to the 'wrong' music in the privacy of one's home was not acceptable if those forms of art somehow expressed a different view of how things ought to be.)

The problem with this private way of dealing with value arguments is that there are many issues for which it doesn't work. We can't help but affect others with many of our value judgements. To continue to use art as way of illustrating this, there are plenty of examples where some art is so contrary to someone's values that they are upset by the very fact of its existence in their society, regardless of whether they have to see it themselves. In a famous example, in 1999 the art exhibition 'Sensation' caused a huge public storm in New York City. The mayor at the time, Rudi Guiliani, threatened to cut off public subsidy to the Brooklyn Museum. The Catholic Archbishop of New York, John O'Connor, called it 'an attack on religion itself'.[4] Neither of them had any intention of actually viewing the artwork at the centre of the row (Chris Ofili's version of the Madonna, which included elephant dung and collages from pornographic magazines; Young, 2005). Instead, their view of what values a society should uphold extended to the principle of whether a museum should ever display such a work.

Therefore we need a third option, a way of resolving arguments where values spill into the public sphere, whether about dung Madonnas, the value of media studies or much more profound matters, without resorting to either authoritarianism or violence. One of the purposes of democratic politics is that it attempts to find such a way. The belief that it is possible for people with different values to co-exist and find workable compromises is at the heart of democracy.

The next step in this argument is to confront an obvious paradox: asserting that democracy is about finding a way to work through differences in values is in itself a value judgement: an 'ought' not an 'is'. Democracy isn't going to help if people aren't prepared to make a prior commitment to the underlying value of democracy itself. This realisation appears to put democracy in rather a weak position. Most people don't spend their time thinking about democratic process and whether or not their society has ways to work through differences. Such concepts are rather abstract. Other feelings about what is right and wrong are likely to be much more immediate, visceral and compelling. Also, if democracy's way of handling value differences is to seek compromise and acceptance, that doesn't sit comfortably with clear judgements about what is right and wrong. The more that the issues of the day provoke such sharp moral feelings, the more that people are likely to value their side of the argument about what is 'right' coming out on top, with attachment to democratic means of getting there coming a rather poor second.

A good illustration of how commitment to democracy can fall away when confronted with a much more immediate and heart-felt set of values is the experience of the US Deep South in the 'Jim Crow' era. The Southern states sat under the federal constitution, with its commitments to equality, free speech and a democratic process. State constitutions, even in segregationist states like Mississippi and South Carolina, used democratic language about government authority being derived from the people. Southern politicians called themselves democrats (with both lower and upper-case 'D') and were some of the most vocal and forthright proponents of an aggressive stance against the dictatorship of the Soviet Union and its repression of democracy in Eastern Europe (Katznelson, 2013).

However, these apparent commitments to democratic principles fell away when confronted with a much more immediate and practical value judgement being made by those leaders: the importance of white supremacy. If African-Americans were able to participate in the political system, they would attack segregation and fundamentally change Southern society. Constrained by the federal courts and also possibly by some desire to retain a veneer of democracy, the measures put in place to stop African-Americans from entering politics were not explicitly racist. Instead, the Southern states had processes that were theoretically universal but in fact had a blatantly discriminatory effect. A favourite strategy was to require people who wished to register to vote to take a test, with a white official committed to racial supremacy able to make a judgement on who had passed (Key, 1949).

The organisation 'Veterans of the Civil Rights Movement' has kept some fantastic examples of these tests. One, that the state of Louisiana used as late as the 1960s, was supposedly a test of literacy but the questions are so ambiguous that the person marking the test (the white supremacist election official) would effectively have had complete discretion to decide who passed and who failed. The test tells the applicant 'above the letter "X" draw a small cross'. Whatever size cross the African-American applicant drew, it could be deemed not small enough, or 'very small' rather than 'small', or whatever was convenient. Perhaps it is not surprising that in 1960 there were several counties in Louisiana where less than 1 per cent of African-American residents were registered to vote.[5]

The Jim Crow era is an extreme case of values driving and perverting an attitude to democracy. There are contrasting examples where democracies have successfully managed fundamental conflicts about values, on issues that people care about much more strongly than they generally do about abstract democratic principles. These cases imply that it is possible for people to hold on to an underlying adherence to democratic values even if the outcomes of democracy are challenging to other values they hold dear.

An example of such a case is the move in many Western countries towards accepting same-sex marriage. What kind of relationship is accepted in society is hugely emotive and speaks to deep-seated value judgements about how people should live. Opposition to mixed-race relationships was in fact one of the most visceral parts of the Jim Crow ideology discussed above. Actual or alleged relationships across racial lines were one of the major triggers of lynching and other white supremacist violence (Beck and Tolney, 1995). Yet same-sex marriage has been introduced in the United States, the United Kingdom, Australia and elsewhere without widespread rejection of democratic decisions or attempts to overturn them through violence.

A detailed account of why it has been possible to move acceptance of same-sex marriage into the mainstream needs to wait until it is possible to take a longer perspective. But the experience so far does illustrate some points about how democratic systems can deal with values. One view of the same-sex marriage debate is that marriage has effectively moved into the category of private value judgements. Are people, in general, simply less bothered about what others do in their private lives? Perhaps a gradual shift has taken place over the generations in what people care about, thereby defusing the argument. If this is right, then the democratic systems we are considering have not shown through the same-sex marriage case that they can cope with disputes about values that have wide public impact. Instead it is merely the case that the public impact of this issue has decreased to a point where it is not big enough to cause trouble.

The Harvard philosopher Michael Sandel makes a compelling counter-argument to this latter view, which has a wider resonance when thinking about the place of values within a democracy. In his 2009 Reith lecture he considered the judgement of the Massachusetts Supreme Court that permitted same-sex marriage. He points out that Chief Justice Margaret Marshall made it clear that the question of what constituted marriage could not be a private one, given that marriage was a formal, legal and public institution. If no-one was bothered about other's private lives, the logical conclusion would be to have no institution of marriage at all, or alternatively to allow any sort of marriage whatsoever, including polygamy or marrying an animal. The only logical position was that the court was making a value judgement about what constituted a relationship that the State of Massachusetts was prepared to endorse (Sandel, 2009).

Many people would not be comfortable with a political system that was so neutral about values that it allowed marriage to be whatever anyone felt like at the time. And it also feels rather a cop-out to just hope that heated debates simply fade away and become private matters so we do not need to talk about them. What about issues where there is no sign that will happen? Abortion in the United States is as controversial now as it was in 1973 when the Supreme Court made its landmark decision in Roe vs Wade that there was a constitutional right to an abortion. It was similarly explosive a century earlier when the New York Society for the Suppression of Vice advocated for the Comstock Law which made it illegal to publish information about abortions (LaMay, 1997). If we don't have democratic processes capable of discussing such issues, there is a risk that the disputes will spill over into abuse and violence.

Values-based language in the political process

So how can democracies pursue this goal of enabling discussions where people have different values, without falling into the trap where people care more about those values than they do about democracy, leading such discussions to undermine the democratic system itself? One part of the answer is in the language that we use for political debate. If democracy is to function effectively as a process for constructive discussion about values, we need to steer a course between two dangerous alternatives.

The first of those is to make political language too technocratic, so we are not honest about where the disagreement is really about values, about an 'ought' not an 'is'. The 'Remain' campaign in the United Kingdom's referendum on membership of the EU has been criticised by many for falling into this mistake. The core Remain message was about economic risk, backed up by statistics on how much income people might forgo as a consequence of economic damage from Brexit. Senior business leaders and economists made fact-based appeals to voters about the future. As subsequent research has shown, the drivers of the vote were to a large degree much more about culture and values. I discuss this issue in more detail in Chapter 6. More generally, political interviews and government publications often focus on the costs of policies, how they will be implemented and their relevance to political campaigning and manoeuvring by parties or individual candidates. None of this speaks to why something matters, what it says about the values of the politician proposing it or how it encapsulates a vision of society.

The other dangerous alternative is to move right away from technocracy towards value-based language, but to do so in a way that is not conducive to a democratic debate that enables different values to co-exist in society. Taking such a route includes rhetoric that denies the validity of contrary views, and in particular that denies their right to be heard as part of the debate. It risks eliminating the space needed for compromise about how different people can get along. Such exclusionary rhetoric has been the staple of demagogues down the ages. It often takes the form of defining the 'people' (the group to whom the demagogue wishes to appeal) in opposition to some 'other' enemy groups in society. These can be racial or religious minorities, or economic classes (either elites or the disadvantaged) or combinations. A crucial aspect of this kind of approach is that the 'other' are defined as not fully part of the society, and therefore not worthy of either protections given by the rule of law or of full rights to participate in the political process (Wodak, 2015).

So what we are looking for is a way of talking about values that is open and genuine, without veering into exclusion or hostility. Politicians and commentators need to talk about why they are doing things, their vision for the good society and what is fair. It is very tempting to do this in bland slogans that do not convey any sense of a choice being made about values. Looking at the titles and slogans of recent election campaigns in the United States and the United Kingdom emphasises how easy it is to fall into content-less vacuity: 'Stronger Together' (Clinton in 2016) 'Believe in America' (Romney in 2012), 'Ambitions for Britain' (Labour in 2001), 'Forward, Together' (Conservatives in 2017 – remarkably similar to the defeated Clinton campaign of seven months earlier). Further back in history there are some examples of slogans that make a very clear value statement. The crucial requirement for such a statement to be meaningful is that it would be possible to disagree with it. Woodrow Wilson campaigned in 1916 under the banner of 'He Kept Us Out Of the War', somewhat ironically in the light of later events. Four years later Warren Harding repeated the line 'Cox and Cocktails' to make the anti-prohibition values of his opponent front and centre of the voters' minds. Such directness at least demonstrates that political leaders recognise that there are real choices and trade-offs between values to be made.[6]

One model that has received a lot of attention as a way of having a reasonable debate where there are hard trade-offs and tensions to be addressed is what is known as 'deliberative democracy' (Dryzek, 2002). This involves bringing together a group of citizens to discuss the options for taking action on a given issue. They are given information, different perspectives and possible policy choices, and take part in a structured process that (hopefully) enables them to come to a conclusion. The idea behind this approach is twofold. First, the direct involvement of citizens enables them to bring their perspectives, values and assumptions to bear on an issue and to test them with those held by others, in a way that simply isn't possible through debates between representatives in a parliament or other assembly. Second, it is hoped that positions emerging from such a process will be accepted as legitimate by the community as a whole. Perhaps people will be more prepared to accept trade-offs, including around their values, if those have been arrived at by a considered process involving their peers.

One recent attempt to tackle an issue with emotive values at its centre occurred recently in the Republic of Ireland. There, a Citizens Assembly (with 100 lay members) considered the vexed question of whether and how to change the Republic's abortion law. The deliberations in the assembly over five weekends led to a set of recommendations and ultimately to the 2018 referendum on changing the abortion provisions in the Irish Constitution. The Assembly did not remove emotive and inflammatory language from the referendum debate, or lead to a position where everyone was happy. This was never going to be possible on something with the level of passionate deeply held views that exist around abortion in Ireland. What it does demonstrate, however, is that structured citizen deliberation can open up possibilities for dealing with the most value-laden issues in an effective way (Whelan, 2018).

Deliberative processes have their place, but they also need a lot of care to establish and are extremely time-consuming. It simply isn't practical for 100 people to spend five weekends debating every values-based question that governments face. Advocates of citizen involvement in decision making point to another approach, known as participatory democracy. Probably the most famous example of this comes from Brazil. In the 1980s the Workers Party there started to develop radical new models of involving citizens in policy making. These experiments stemmed from a belief that their purpose was not just to win power under the current system but to change it. In 1989 Olivo Dutre was elected mayor of Porto Alegre and launched a process called 'participatory budgeting'. This aimed to involve citizens directly in making spending choices and trade-offs, deciding where to deploy a limited pot of money. By the early 2000s some 50,000 people were taking part in the process, out of a population of 1.5 million (Shah, 2007). Participatory budgeting, and similar deliberative methods applied to other issues, have now spread around the world. In a more recent example, the city of Paris has begun what it claims is the largest participatory budget process in the world (Veron, 2018), allocating at least 5 per cent of the city's capital expenditure from 2014 to 2020. In a particularly interesting twist on the model, the Parisian system reserves a portion of the funds for schoolchildren to decide on investment projects in their schools (better equipment, more activities and so on). This last innovation has the dual aim of achieving better and more widely accepted decisions about the school budget and developing a habit of participation at a young age.

These models can operate at a frequency and scale that has not yet been attempted with purely deliberative approaches. There is, however, a trade-off with the depth and difficulty of issue that they can address. Budget decisions do invoke values (such as 'who deserves what?' 'what outcomes do we as a city value most'?) but do not necessarily get into the kinds of moral issues, such as abortion law, which can be most difficult for democracies to handle.

It is possible that digital platforms could make deliberation or participation quicker and easier, opening up a wider set of scenarios where each of these tools become viable. However it is less clear that technology will solve another problem that the two approaches both face: that of inclusion. The World Bank (2008a) noted that Porto Alegre has often struggled to enable the most economically marginalised citizens to access and influence the budget process. This is simply an example of a wider point: it will never be possible to include everyone and every perspective. Looking at deliberative forums, Muers (2004) demonstrated there is no guarantee that making a deliberative forum a bit more inclusive will move the answer closer to something that everyone would accept, if the inclusion remains anything short of perfect. It all depends who you add in and how their views relate to the rest of society. If by making a forum more inclusive you add some extremists, that won't help achieve overall legitimacy and consensus. Deliberative and participatory tools are, therefore, like all the other democratic methods: they can help achieve a consensus around values, but only if used in the right context and in the right way.

Conclusion

Overall, then, questions of values lie at the centre of the political process and are a key reason why issues become political at all. All societies need a way to resolve questions of what 'ought' to be the case, rather than debates about the facts of what 'is'. Democracy can do this, and reasoned debate about how to co-exist with people who share some but not all values is one of the purposes of a democratic system. However, that purpose will always come under pressure when the values at play are more important to people than supporting democracy itself. The need to navigate this challenge, through careful use of language and creativity about institutional design, is another reason why culture and values are central concerns for policy makers.

5

Governments can't help affecting culture

We have seen in the previous chapters how important culture and values are to determining whether a policy works and whether it is seen as legitimate, and the role of politics in managing values-based conflicts. These discussions leave open a rather large question: can governments actually affect culture and values at all? If they can't, then the options for the policy maker to address the issues raised so far are limited. Taking culture seriously would become a matter of managing what exists, rather than shaping it pro-actively. This chapter addresses this question of whether governments can affect culture and values, and also whether they should.

Can governments affect culture and values?

The 2003 film *Good Bye, Lenin!* was a huge hit, making around $80 million at the box office and winning numerous awards.[1] It told the story of a family in Berlin struggling to cope with the level of change and dislocation brought about by the fall of the Berlin Wall and imminent German unification. The difference in culture in the two Germanies comes out powerfully through the humour in the film. The division of Germany created a natural experiment in what impact governments can have on culture and values. Where there had been one country before 1949 there were now two, run by regimes with completely different sets of values and contrasting world-views. Did the democratic capitalist regime in West Germany lead to the population holding different values to those found in the Communist East?

The 'experiment' in Germany was particularly extreme because of the nature of the East German regime. It was a totalitarian system, which regarded the mindsets and values of citizens as not just something the state could influence but as a domain in which it absolutely had to take a central role. As Service (2007) argues, this desire for control over every aspect of life, culture and values as much as laws and institutions was a hallmark of Communist regimes in Eastern Europe and elsewhere. The East German state pulled every possible lever to influence the way citizens thought and acted. The official purposes of East German social policy were set out by the DDR's Institute for Sociology and Social Policy in 1985 and placed values firmly within the ambit of the state (Scharf, 1988).

This extremely far reaching view of the scope of appropriate state control came across in many fields. For example, the school curriculum was heavily politicised, teaching East German schoolchildren a world-view and set of values in line with Communist ideology. Rodden (2009: 168) studied the textbooks provided to East German children of primary school age. He found that a 'significantly greater part of them was devoted to ideological claims that were usually advanced in far sharper, blunter terms than in their western counterparts'. Many of the stories in the books were aimed at glorifying Communist heroes (Marx, Stalin and so forth) as well as contemporary East German leaders, holding them out as role models of an ideal life. Cultural and sporting events were another tool that the East German state used to influence culture. Such occasions were managed with political and ideological goals at the forefront, sport in particular being seen as having the cultural purpose of national glorification and demonstrating the strength of the socialist system (Hardman and Naul, 2002).

So did these devoted efforts to create a distinctive Communist culture in East Germany have any lasting effects, or was it instead the case that once the formal economic and political rules changed dramatically, underlying culture and values rapidly came into line with those in the West? The unusual situation created by division and reunification of Germany encouraged several scholars to test differences between the two Germanies and whether they endured over time. Alesina and Fuchs-Schundeln (2006) even called their study 'Good bye Lenin (or not?)'. They found that significant differences in values between East and West Germany persisted well after the reunification process was complete. East Germans included in their study retained much stronger preferences for redistribution and state control of the economy. These differences in values were present even when they controlled for economic circumstances (and therefore whether someone was personally likely to benefit from such policies). The study also demonstrated that the effect on values was stronger the longer someone had lived in East Germany, and the authors estimated that it would take one or two generations for the impact of the East German state's policies on values to disappear.

The German experience does, therefore, demonstrate that governments can affect values. This is perhaps not surprising given the huge efforts made by the East German government, and totalitarian Communist regimes are an extreme case. This book is more focused on helping policy makers based in liberal democracies to operate more effectively. Without access to the tools of state-controlled media, mass rallies giving ideological messages and minute control over the content of school textbooks and other cultural outputs, do policy makers still have the ability to influence culture?

It is clear that many liberal democratic governments believe that they do. When I walk into my son's primary school in West London, almost the first thing I see is a large poster on the main window proudly stating that this is a 'values-based school'. A little further down the main corridor is a wall display about 'British values', with comments from children throughout the school about what the various values mean to them. British values were included in the school curriculum in England at the express direction of government and with the intention of influencing how children think and what they see as acceptable. The relevant Department for Education guidance says that schools should 'actively promote fundamental British values' and also 'promote pupils' spiritual, social, moral and cultural development' (Department for Education, 2014). The contemporary British approach is certainly nowhere near what the East Germans were doing but it is still an ambitious programme. It is part of what Lander (2016) describes as a 'muscular' approach to a particular form of liberalism and also a desire for schools to contribute to a national security agenda.

A different example from another liberal Western European state is the French government's approach to promotion of the French language. Successive French governments have taken the position that the language is a valuable part of French culture and that it is potentially under threat from the growing international use of English. They have also argued that the state is both able to and entitled to promote it. This promotion takes place both through soft power (for example funding and encouraging education in French in other countries) and much harder levers within France itself (for example mandating the use of French in commercial communications; Ma, 2017).

Should governments affect culture and values?

So governments in liberal democratic societies believe that they can affect culture and values in a way that is consistent with their overall position in society and the sources of their legitimacy. Should they do so? There is a strand of criticism which says such efforts are not really either liberal or democratic. This argument is, first, that a liberal government is meant to reflect the preferences of its citizens rather than operating as an independent or semi-independent actor trying to drive them in a certain direction. If values and culture start to shift (for example, towards people putting less value on the preservation of the French language) shouldn't a liberal state accept and facilitate that rather than attempting to stand in the way or reverse change? A second argument focuses on the 'democracy' part of liberal democracy. This is that by trying to shape culture and values the state risks affecting the power dynamics in society and will skew debate. Free, open and undistorted debate is an essential component of a functioning democracy. Could the very process of such debate be affected by policies that are directed at altering culture, especially culture around democratic practice? The 'British values' example mentioned above has been very controversial, and forms of both of these arguments have been made to object to the policy. Lander (2016) objects to 'blatant reinforcement of teachers as instruments of the state within a liberal democracy'(p 274) and that debate is being skewed towards 'nostalgic imperialist constructions of Britishness' (p 276). The other contributions to the same journal volume as Lander's piece demonstrate considerable concern, from different starting points, with the implications of a liberal state pursuing this sort of policy.

There are two main counter-arguments to these objections that we should consider. The first is, at its simplest, to argue that liberalism is not a neutral ideology that allows complete divergence of views and does require some degree of 'muscularity' to maintain it. In this view, a liberal state will not remain necessarily remain liberal by doing nothing about the values that underpin its operation. Instead it can be argued that those values are a positive choice rather than simply the absence of alternative values. In Chapter 4 on the place of values in democracy we discussed the work of Michael Sandel. He argues for a 'public philosophy' (Sandel, 2005) where state, citizens and civic institutions create 'an animating vision of the good society, and of the shared obligations of citizenship' (2005: 3). In this view of the world the state cannot be a neutral actor as it has a part to play in sustaining the values that underpin the whole system of which it is a part. An 'animating vision' is unlikely to appear by accident. Whether or not the kinds of activities undertaken by the British and French states in the examples above would be supported by Sandel or a follower of his thinking as part of creating such a vision is a moot point. Anyone who follows Bryan and Revill (2016) in arguing that the British values agenda puts pressure on teachers to become part of a more intrusive national security apparatus in the United Kingdom would surely argue that in this case the state has gone too far. Regardless of the merits of this specific case, the wider principle that a liberal state may need to be active in developing liberalism and helping sustain the values that underpin it is an important one.

The second counter-argument takes a different tack. It doesn't rely on an underlying theory of the state in the way that Sandel's work does. Instead it starts from a different classic philosophical question: the act/omission distinction. The *Oxford Dictionary of Philosophy* says that this question is about whether 'it makes an ethical difference whether an agent actively intervenes to bring about a result, or omits to act in circumstances in which it is foreseen that as a result of the omission the same result occurs' (Blackburn, 1994). The same entry goes on to explain this with an example: if I am responsible for providing you with food but I do not, and you starve to death, is this the moral equivalent of killing you by some direct violent action? The most famous example of using the act/omission issue to investigate a philosophical issue came with Philippa Foot's famous 'trolley problem' (Foot, 1967). Foot posed a thought experiment where a runaway railway trolley was careering down a track and heading for a junction. On one branch of the track five people were working and would all be killed by the trolley if it passed that way. On the other there was just one worker. The points were set so that, absent any intervention, the trolley would head for the five workers. If you, as a bystander, can switch the points so the single person dies instead, could you be said to have 'killed' them in a way that by not operating the lever you would not have 'killed' the five?

What has this got to do with the state affecting culture and values? The point is that objectors to the idea of liberal democratic states trying to affect those phenomena face an act/ omission distinction. It seems clear, from the evidence that we have considered, that states can affect culture and values. Pushing the logic a bit further, modern democratic states employ millions of people and generally spend 30–40 per cent of GDP. At this scale of impact on a society, is hard to imagine how the state can avoid affecting culture and values in some way, even if it doesn't have policies that are explicitly intended to do so. Therefore the choice is not between affecting culture and not affecting it, but between doing so by conscious action and doing so by omission. It seems to me that affecting culture by omission is not more true to a liberal ideal but is instead potentially careless. If the state's impact on culture is not considered consciously, there must be a risk that impact is more harmful to overall liberal values than would otherwise be the case.

Even if we accept either or both of these counter-arguments, it is right to be cautious about how governments may try to push culture in certain directions. The controversy over the British values policy is appropriate and healthy: it is not clear cut where the right balance lies between trying to do nothing and thereby affecting culture by accident and a heavy-handed approach that ends up distorting proper democratic development. Each society needs to find out where the balance is that works in that context and to adapt that over time. This process is more likely to take place effectively if governments are explicit and conscious about how they might affect culture and values. To do so they will need to have a dialogue with other actors in society about how the government's impact manifests itself and what is or isn't working, as well as being aware of the policy tools involved and considering the capabilities needed to use them well. Part Three of this book considers some of those tools in more detail. An approach that lets the impact of government take place by omission feels to me less honest and more risky.

Conclusion

We can see from history that governments can affect culture and values. The totalitarian states of the Eastern Bloc are an extreme example, but the German case in particular provides strong evidence for the impact the state can have on mindsets, priorities and sense of fairness. Liberal democratic states also try to manage culture and values, with different approaches and degrees of success. Even if they do not have explicit policies to do so, large modern governments cannot help but have an impact on the societies of which they are a part. Managing that impact consciously, rather than by omission, is part of putting culture and values at the heart of policy making.

PART TWO

How culture and values shape the political system

Part One of this book set out four reasons why culture and values matter for public policy. This second part moves the focus more to the political sphere. As any policy maker knows, the political context is an essential part of determining how policy is made and delivered. Politics sets the environment within which policy makers operate, determining what is possible and what is deemed important. As will be clear from the following two chapters, culture and values have a direct impact on politics. Therefore, they drive policy outcomes via the political sphere as well as directly.

The two following chapters focus on two aspects of the political system. Chapter 6 looks at voters and voting behaviour, and the way culture and values contribute to explaining them. Chapter 7 is focused on how political systems deliver accountability, and how that is affected by culture and values. The discussion in this part concentrates on democratic political systems. How voters behave is clearly rather less important in countries where there are no elections or they are manipulated in such a way that what voters actually think and do is irrelevant to the outcome. Political accountability does, of course, exist in non-democratic systems. However, the mechanisms through which it works are different, and would need separate treatment outside the scope of this book.

6

Values voters

Voting is a fundamental part of a democratic system. The whole premise of democracy is that governments derive their right to rule through being freely chosen by citizens. How votes translate into government formation and then government action depends on electoral systems, party systems and institutional design. There is a vast literature that addresses these factors (for example, Ware, 1996) which I will not cover in detail here. The fundamental principle of open elections remains common to all those different democratic systems. From the Chartists to the Suffragettes, to American civil rights activists and the demonstrators of the Arab Spring, people have been prepared to suffer hardship and death for the right to vote.

To understand how voting feeds through into first government creation and then policy, we need to look at why people vote the way they do. What factors can we use to explain the decision that they make as they pull the handle on a voting machine, or mark an 'X' on the ballot paper with (in my experience in the United Kingdom) a short and very blunt pencil? This chapter looks into voting behaviour, and how it is affected by culture and values.

Do policies determine how people vote?

In any British general election campaign, the party manifestos are a central theme. In 2017 there was huge excitement in the media when the Labour manifesto was leaked to the media before the formal launch.[1] Journalists could pull out whatever aspects they were interested in and highlight them before the party leadership was able to set its own narrative. At 126 pages, with policies on everything from the future of the United Kingdom's independent nuclear deterrent to what percentage of their income from television rights the Premier League football clubs should invest into grassroots sport (Labour Party, 2017), there was plenty of opportunity to create stories. In this and in other recent elections, entrepreneurial and tech-savvy citizens have created websites where you could answer questions about your policy preferences and the site would match your answers to party manifestos and recommend which party was closest to your position.

Underlying the media focus on large policy heavy manifestos, and the creation of the policy choice websites, is a major assumption about how voters behave. This is that people choose which party or which candidate to vote for on the basis of the policies that they put forward. Voters look at the policies on offer, choose which set comes closest to their preferences on the issues they deem most important, and decide accordingly. Such a model seems rational and in keeping with the idea that the government does what voters have chosen it to do, which is a basic tenet of democratic theory. One of the most famous explanations of this assumption and its effect on policy is Downs' 'median voter theory' (Downs, 1957). The theory holds that on any given issue there will be a distribution of preferences among the voters. Political parties will try to adopt policy positions that give them the greatest chance of winning more votes than the alternative parties. Downs argues that this will pull parties towards the position of the median voter. Any other strategy risks allowing another party to win by moving more towards the median themselves. The median position may well not be the one favoured by the most people (the median is not the same as the mode), but political competition will still move parties in that direction. The next step in the argument is to assert that the median voter is likely to have relatively moderate preferences, and so parties will tend towards moderate policy positions towards the centre of the ideological spectrum, assuming they are motivated by the prospect of electoral success.

We will look later at whether parties do in fact tend to converge on the mid-point as Downs' model would predict.

However staying at the theoretical level, we first need to test whether it makes sense to assume that voters do make decisions on the basis of policy at all. If they do not, then the median voter effect is irrelevant anyway. What happens if those choices at the ballot box are actually driven by something else?

Many politicians behave as if policy is a critical driver of voting. For example, they put considerable effort into telling people that election manifestos have been implemented. In the winter of 2012–13 I was working in the Economic and Domestic Secretariat in the UK Cabinet Office. This rather esoterically-named unit was responsible for coordinating domestic policy across government, resolving disputes between different government departments and supporting the Prime Minister and the Cabinet Secretary in creating and delivering a coherent agenda. During this period the country was run by a coalition between the Conservatives and the Liberal Democrats. As part of their agreement to enter coalition the two parties had drawn up a detailed document called 'The Programme for Government' (HM Government, 2010). This set out public agreement between the two parties on priorities across the full range of government policy. That winter the coalition partners decided they wanted to make a public statement of the progress they had made against their priorities, halfway through the five-year term for which they had been elected. My team and I were in charge of coordinating this statement, pulling together updates from different government departments on what had been done against each of the (roughly: it depended on exactly what counted) 350 policy commitments contained within the Programme. We fed the updates into a review process led by Oliver Letwin for the Conservatives and Danny Alexander for the Liberal Democrats. In long meetings, often fuelled by pizza, in Oliver's grand office overlooking Horse Guards Parade in central London they went through all the information and decided how to pull it together into a clear and comprehensive account of the government's achievements.

The result was a publication known as 'the Mid-Term Review' (HM Government, 2013). It was nothing if not comprehensive, covering what had been done to make progress with implementation of all of those detailed policies. The government clearly felt it was worth devoting the time of lots of civil servants, and two of the ministers most important to the smooth functioning of government, to publishing this account. It would be a strange thing to do if policy implementation was not important in determining the political success of the government (as ultimately measured by elections).

When you look at the detail of the Mid-Term Review, however, questions start to emerge. Most of it talks about announcements made, new policies established, legislation introduced. Very little gives hard evidence of any real change that would affect ordinary voters. Partly this is because the coalition was only two years old, and change that people can see in their day-to-day lives takes time. But it is also partly because many of those policies would never have the consequences that were intended. This is not a particular criticism of the policy agenda and approach held by that government, but a more general point. As set out in Chapter 2, policy initiatives formulated in (for example) grand offices overlooking Horse Guards Parade look rather different when they hit the reality of under-pressure front-line staff trying to fit them into existing organisational cultures and structures. As that chapter showed, these 'street-level bureaucrats' change the ways that policies are implemented or whether they are implemented at all. If a policy may well not be implemented, it would make little sense for a voter to make their choice because they like the policy. Why choose a government because it says it is going to do something when that isn't actually going to happen, or at least not in the way promised?

There is good evidence that such scepticism about whether or not policies promised by politicians in election manifestos will be implemented is pretty widespread among voters. On an anecdotal basis, we have all probably had conversations or seen news footage where people routinely say 'politicians can't be trusted to keep their promises'. There is also more formal evidence that such beliefs exist. For example, a study in Sweden found that only 18 per cent of people agreed with the statement 'elected members of Parliament try to keep their election promises' (Naurin, 2011). The study also found that a good proportion of policies were implemented at least in some form. Looking at South Korea, Rhu (2017) found that 87 per cent of younger voters were sceptical that politicians would keep their promises. Findings like these imply that voters may be even more mistrustful than the reality of partial implementation, affected by front-line challenge and culture, would warrant.

So most policies are not fully implemented, and voters do not generally believe that they will be. These findings cast serious doubt on whether voters do make their choices on the basis of policy, as it would not be rational to do so. There are further arguments that reinforce such doubts. The first is that even if voters did believe that policies would be implemented, is it plausible for people to obtain and act on the level of policy knowledge that would be required? Going back to that 2017 Labour manifesto, with its 126 pages of detailed policy prescriptions, it does not seem realistic that anyone outside a tiny group of politicians and commentators would be aware of, let alone understand, a tiny fraction of the content. It is easy for people like me (and, I suspect, many readers of this book) to forget that not everyone plays close attention to the minutiae of policy and politics. I remember an experiment that BBC News conducted a few years ago in central London, where they projected images of senior members of the British Cabinet onto an advertising billboard and asked passers-by if they knew who they were. Once the journalist got beyond the Prime Minister and Chancellor of the Exchequer, very few people could put any names to faces. The polling firm YouGov did a similar test in a more scientific way in 2015, and found that (for example) only 19 per cent of people could recognise the Shadow Chancellor and 15 per cent the Education Secretary.[2]

This limited knowledge of politicians reflects a wider point: most people are too busy with their personal and family lives and their other interests to engage with news and current affairs even in a broad sense. Another polling company (Populus) routinely asks people in the United Kingdom what news story they noticed in the previous week.[3] Taking one week in December 2018, when arguments about the United Kingdom's plans to leave the European Union were at one of their periodic peaks, roughly half the interview sample couldn't recall any news stories at all (Populus, 2018a). In April 2018 the firm reviewed their polling data for the year so far (Populus, 2018b). This found that it was very rare for any political story to be recalled by more than a third of their sample in a given week. The bar here is pretty low – simply recalling the story rather than testing whether that recall was accurate, or the extent to which anyone actually understood anything about the content. It seems safe to assume that the proportion achieving those greater levels of comprehension would be much lower still. More academic research has come to a similar conclusion, finding that even among people who watch television news (in itself a minority) they can often remember very little of the content (Gunther, 2015).

Looking beyond immediate political news, we can look at knowledge and understanding of political institutions overall. Do people, generally, understand how politics in their country works? Achen and Bartels (2016) looked at this in the United States and considered survey evidence taken over a period of more than 50 years. This showed an impressive lack of even basic knowledge about the country's political institutions. They note that in 1952 only 44 per cent of Americans could name even one branch of government. Looking at survey results over time, they conclude that while knowledge of political institutions is linked to levels of education, and overall education levels have increased, there has not been a corresponding rise in overall knowledge. They conclude that the data indicates that the variance in political knowledge is now greater but the average is very similar: more people know a lot than was the case a generation ago, but more also now know virtually nothing.

Another reason not to focus on policy detail is that much of political leadership is about responding to what British Prime Minister Harold Macmillan is alleged to have called 'events, dear boy, events'.[4] Nobody can predict what they will have to deal with when they are in government, except for the near certainty that it will involve unexpected scenarios. A manifesto tells voters little about how someone will respond to an economic shock, a war or a natural disaster. Given that doing so in an effective way is one of the most important functions of government, it would therefore make sense for voters to look for other ways to inform the choice they make at election time.

Therefore it seems that voters are behaving in a rational way, and are not using policy as a primary way of making choices. They believe that many policies will not be implemented, because they mistrust politicians and because they recognise the real implementation challenges that inevitably get in the way. They also recognise that detailed policy proposals may not be a good guide to how someone will respond to crises and other unexpected events. It is therefore perfectly sensible not to invest time and effort in understanding complex policies and political systems, when there are so many competing calls on everyone's time and attention.

This conclusion makes it very unlikely that people in general vote on the basis of policy proposals. A final example that illustrates this point comes from the British general election of 1983. The Labour manifesto for that election has often been called 'the longest suicide note in history' for its strong left-wing positioning. However, if you took the issues voters said were most important and then which party they also said had the best policies on those issues, you would have expected a landslide victory for the Labour Party. Instead, Margaret Thatcher won the largest majority of any government for nearly 40 years (Butler and Kavanagh, 1984).

Do culture and values determine how people vote?

If policy detail doesn't work as a model for looking at voting, do culture and values offer a more plausible account? We can tackle this question in two ways. There is a set of academic research that looks in general at the drivers of political choice from the perspective of culture and values. Then there is work on what factors predicted voting behaviour on specific occasions. As I set out in the Introduction, there has been considerable research that addresses this point around the particular instances of the United Kingdom's 2016 referendum on leaving the European Union and on the election of Donald Trump as US president in the same year.

Looking first at the more general work, a good example is Barnea and Schwartz's study (1998) of how fundamental values that people hold affect how they vote. They used a set of value types based on research in 47 countries around fundamental motivating values in different cultural contexts (Schwartz, 1992). Schwartz regards these values as cognitive representations of desirable, abstract, trans-situational goals that serve as guiding principles in people's lives. The values include tradition (respect, commitment, and acceptance of the customs and ideas that traditional culture or religion provide), benevolence (preservation and enhancement of the welfare of people with whom one is in frequent personal contact) and universalism (understanding, appreciation, tolerance, and protection for the welfare of all people and for nature; Barnea and Schwartz, 1998: 19). They then applied these values to the context of elections in Israel. They concluded that 'the results support the assumption that value priorities predispose individuals to vote for particular political parties' (1998: 36). Seven of the value types showed a significant association with voting behaviour. They also looked at how values intersected with demographic factors that had previously been shown to affect voting in Israel (namely age, ethnic group and education level). They found that values were more important than those factors, but only in explaining the differences in voter choice between parties that were clearly ideologically distinct (not always the case in Israel's multi-party system; Barnea and Schwartz, 1998: 35).

Capara et al (2006) conducted a similar study, looking at Italy rather than Israel. They also used Schwartz's (1992) set of value types, and added another set of factors that covered personality traits (based on McCrae and John, 1992). This was in part to test whether values or non-cognitive personality traits had more significant explanatory power in analysis of voter behaviour.[5] The study concluded that five of the value types had a significant correlation with how someone voted, and values added significantly to the predictive power of a model when added to demographic variables, as with the Israeli study. On the particular point about the relative importance of values and personality type, the authors conclude that their analysis shows that 'values subsume traits in predicting political orientation' (Capara et al, 2006: 24).

These studies, then, provide good evidence for the importance of values in determining how people vote. Another set of research has argued that factors lying even deeper within us than fundamental values are also important. This research focuses on hereditary elements. In his bestseller *The Righteous Mind*, Jonathan Haidt (2012) argues that political behaviour is driven by views on the importance of six basic values (care, liberty, fairness, loyalty, authority and sanctity). He then argues further that the strength of our attachment to those values is to a large degree (but not entirely) inherited. He uses twin studies as evidence to suggest that between a third and a half of political behaviour is inherited. Fundamental basic values are not something we choose, they are part of who we are, as much as accent or even hair colour. If these values are so deep-set within us, it is perhaps not surprising if they drive the way we choose who runs our country and makes the most important decisions.

Another set of work has looked specifically at what explains why some people are willing to support authoritarian political leaders (Feldman and Stenner, 1997; Stenner, 2005). This work identifies 'authoritarian predispositions' (Feldman and Stenner, 1997: 741) that are activated into political support for authoritarianism by perceptions of external threat (for example increased ethnic minority population in a locality). These predispositions are fundamental personality characteristics that are present from a young age. Crucially for this analysis, Feldman and Stenner use value-statements as one of their main proxies for such conditions. In particular they find that cultural assumptions about child-rearing are a strong predictor of potential support for authoritarianism, measured by the extent to which a respondent agrees with the statement 'Order and respect for authority are the most important virtues a child should learn' (Feldman and Stenner, 1997).

The cases of Brexit and Trump

Two election results in 2016 sent shockwaves through the Anglophone world and more widely. First, on 23 June, the United Kingdom voted to leave the European Union. Then on 8 November, Donald Trump was elected as the 45th President of the United States. Both results were a surprise to the majority of pundits, and betting markets had made 'Remain' and Hillary

Clinton strong favourites. Journalists, other commentators and academics immediately started trying to find explanations of what happened.

Starting with Brexit, much of the narrative immediately became about so-called 'left behind areas'.[6] British pundits may have been swayed towards this because the first inclination of the coming upset on referendum night was the huge pro-Leave vote in Sunderland, a quintessential deprived post-industrial city. Poverty, limited economic opportunity and, in particular, the stagnation of real wages and living standards in the United Kingdom since the 2008 financial crash are all potential explanatory variables. There has been an outpouring of articles with titles such as 'In Brexit-on-Sea, the left-behind still want out'[7] 'The suffering caused by austerity helped fuel Brexit'[8] and 'There'll be an uprising: Hartlepool and life as a Brexit town',[9] as interviewing Brexit supporters in small northern or coastal towns has become a new and thriving journalistic genre.

The researchers wrestling with understanding Brexit have, however, also had to deal with another set of data. This is the strong Leave vote in places very different from Sunderland. Several wealthy local authorities in Southern England also recorded strong majorities for Leave, while major cities with high concentrations of poverty such as Liverpool and Newcastle did not. Some data indicates that the 'typical' leave voter on one definition was in fact middle class and lived in Southern England (Alabrese et al, 2019). Jump and Michell (2020) analysed the relationship between deprivation and Leave voting using the most geographically-detailed data available. They found that the relationship between deprivation and high Leave voting was driven by education levels, and once education and occupational composition of the population were controlled for the relationship became negative.

Demographic factors are clearly part of any explanation of the Brexit vote. But there is strong evidence that values are also an important component of the story. Kaufman (2017) assessed the impact on voting in the referendum of values that are known to have a link to political choice (including a question about child-rearing similar to that used by Feldman and Stenner in the work mentioned above). He also compared the importance of values to that of income. On the child-rearing point, Kaufman's work asked whether people thought it was more important for a child to be 'considerate' or 'well-mannered'. Across the income spectrum, people who said 'well-mannered' were 20–25 percentage points more likely to have voted 'Leave' in the referendum.[10] This difference was roughly five times the difference found when looking at income levels alone, which were barely statistically significant. The relationship between values and the referendum vote is even starker using a different question about values: whether someone supported re-introduction of the death penalty. When controlled for age, gender, education level and region of residence, the people most opposed to the death penalty on a five-point scale were only 20 per cent likely to have voted 'Leave', compared to a 75 per cent likelihood for those taking the position most in favour. As Kaufman concludes 'Values, not income, determined how people voted' (Kaufman, 2017: 20).

Moving to the election of President Trump, we find a similar contest between two possible explanations. One is the 'economic insecurity' thesis. This view emphases how changes to industrial structures in Western economies, the decline of organised labour and increasing relative returns to capital as opposed to labour have led to rising job insecurity and stagnant real incomes, and that Trump was elected in response to these factors. The other is the 'cultural backlash' thesis, explaining Trump's election in terms of a response to progressive cultural shifts on issues including gender and race equality (Inglehart and Norris, 2016).

As with the Brexit case, there has been a strong strain of writing about Trump's election that focuses on the economic thesis, and especially its resonance in areas left behind by economic change. Trump won the election in part because of his narrow victories in Pennsylvania, Michigan and Wisconsin: states heavily affected by industrial decline and which had maintained a long prior streak of voting for Democratic candidates. The industrial Mid-West was home to a large number of counties that switched from supporting Barack Obama in 2012 to supporting Trump four years later. Over 30 percent of Wisconsin counties fell into this category.[11] Some of the swings in this region were dramatic, such as in Howard County in North-East Iowa, which saw a 42 percentage point swing between the two elections.[12] Books such as J D Vance's *Hillbilly Elegy* (2016) and Amy Goldstein's *Janesville* (2017) became popular in the wake of the election and delved into the communities most affected by economic change.

The dramatic electoral swings, and the compelling stories of economic change, need to be balanced against evidence that points more towards the cultural backlash thesis. The first piece of evidence to consider is whether Trump voters were indeed more economically marginalised. When looking at this issue in the context of the United States, it is important to disentangle racial differences: across all income levels black and minority ethnic voters are more likely to vote Democratic. Kaufman (2017) extended his Brexit vote analysis to the United States. He asked people to rate their enthusiasm for Trump on a scale from 0–10. Looking at white voters only, he found that wealthier voters overall gave Trump a 0.5 point *higher* score. No evidence here, then, of the economically marginalised driving his support.

Another study looked to put Trump's success in the context of support for other populist politicians in Europe (Inglehart and Norris, 2016, 2018). Are there similarities between the factors that drove voters to support leaders like Geert Wilders in the Netherlands and Marie Le Pen in France and those seen in the 2016 Presidential race? The work concluded that measures of values provided a consistent predictor of support for these populist politicians, and overall 'the most consistent evidence supporting the cultural backlash thesis' (Inglehart and Norris, 2016: 1). Looking at Trump specifically, it seemed that a strong predictor of support for him was views around political culture, especially whether it was desirable to have a strong leader with few checks and balances. The authors also noted that this view was much more prevalent in voters without a college degree, reinforcing a link found elsewhere (including in the work by Jump and Michell cited above) between education levels and the set of values most likely to predict support for populist agendas.

This evidence pointing towards cultural and value-based explanations for Trump's victory is not surprising when we look at his rhetoric on the campaign trail. Much of it evoked symbols with powerful cultural rather than economic resonance.

The best example is his use of the loaded and much-analysed phrase 'America First'. For example, in his inauguration speech in January 2017 the new president said 'From this day forward, a new vision will govern our land. From this moment on, it's going to be America First.'[13] Sarah Churchwell (2018) analysed the history and cultural connotations of the phrase 'America First' from its origins in the early 20th century. She shows that it started as a bland and almost content-less phrase used by mainstream politicians (Woodrow Wilson being the first notable example) but very rapidly became associated with a particular cultural milieu. This culture was white, rural, patriarchal Protestantism, characterised by opposition to immigration from anywhere apart from Northern Europe and support for prohibition. She also demonstrates that the slogan was enthusiastically adopted by the Ku Klux Klan when that organisation was revived first in Georgia in 1915 and then across the United States in the years that followed. It was then, famously, used by Charles Lindbergh in his campaigns for accommodation between the United States and Germany in the 1930s. President Trump may or may not have been aware of the specific historical uses of 'America First'. Either way though it seems implausible that he, or at least his speech writers, were not conscious of the cultural trappings that it would evoke and the particular view of American values and priorities that have long been attached to it. An appeal based primarily on economics would, surely, not employ such a highly charged term.

The debate about the causes of those two dramatic electoral upsets in 2016 will continue, and a pure binary division between 'economic' and 'values-based' explanations is too simplistic. Values and economic position are not entirely independent variables. As Iversen and Soskice (2019) argue, certain values are associated with certain roles in the economy. In their work this emerges most significantly as a link between success in knowledge-intensive roles in advanced capitalist economies and an open cosmopolitan value set. Looking specifically at the United Kingdom, Jennings and Stoker (2016, 2017) argue that there has been what they call a 'bifurcation' of politics that can be seen in the geography of the Brexit results, but that economic and cultural factors on the two sides of this divide overlap. There is a clear divide in values, as discussed above, but also in the roles people play in the economy. In a similar vein to Iversen and Soskice, Jennings and Stoker (2017: 359) identify 'cosmopolitan' industries, thereby tying economic structures and value-systems together.

New data and new analysis will undoubtedly throw more light in the years to come. The evidence so far does indicate strongly that culture and values had a critical role to play, even if they cannot be entirely separated from economic conditions. Economic policy change may be needed as part of the response to those votes, and the powerful testimony gathered in the books and articles mentioned above cannot be ignored. However, policy makers struggling with their response to a changed political landscape need to recognise the importance of values in how people made their choices. Policies that do not recognise this factor are unlikely to be adequate.

Specific policies as value signals

It is clear from the discussion above that it is theoretically sound to believe that sensible voters would not make their choices as a result of weighing up competing packages of policies. There is also good evidence that underlying culture and values of various types are powerful tools in explaining voter choice. These conclusions leave us with a dilemma: if policy is not important, why on earth do political parties put so much effort into developing it and talking about it? The 126-page Labour manifesto mentioned above must have had some purpose.

There are some reasons for developing detailed policy that have nothing to do with the voters that it is (ostensibly) aimed at. Creating a manifesto is partly about completing an internal process for a political party of agreeing what it will prioritise and resolving disputes between factions. The huge length and detail of that 2017 Labour document may in part be down to this. It was the first comprehensive statement of policy drawn up since Jeremy Corbyn and his left-wing allies took control of the party, and so presented an opportunity to impress their authority and agenda on the party more widely. The platforms agreed at national conventions by political parties in the United States perform a similar function, operating as the grounds for sorting out disputes between party factions as much as attempts to craft coherent and compelling public messages. The 1923 Democratic Convention provides an extreme example of this tendency in US party conventions. The whole convention process nearly disintegrated amid arguments between different party factions about whether to include platform language critical of the Ku Klux Klan. As a result it took 103 ballots to select a candidate, who unsurprisingly ended up being comprehensively defeated (Murray, 1976). In systems where coalition governments are common, manifestos perform a function in signalling to other parties about priorities ahead of possible negotiations on forming a new administration. (Daubler, 2012, found this to be a significant factor in Irish election manifestos.)

Internal party management aside, policy statements do still play a role in the appeal to voters, just not one that relies on those voters having a detailed understanding of the policy or indeed an expectation that it will be delivered. Instead, policy statements can be used as an indication of the overall values and approach advocated by the candidate in question. Going back to the 2016 Presidential election we can find an excellent example of this. Anyone with even a passing interest in the campaign will remember the huge rallies held by Donald Trump, crowned with Make America Great cap-wearing supporters chanting 'Build the Wall! Build the Wall!'. Candidate Trump made a commitment to build the wall and an equally firm assertion that the Mexican government would pay for it. The Mexican-funded border wall was his signature policy position.

On Inauguration Day in 2017, the CBS broadcasting network commissioned a poll on people's views on their new president (CBS, 2017). Among other things, the poll asked about people's confidence in this famous commitment to build a wall and get Mexico to pay for it. Only 14 per cent of respondents believed that it would happen as promised. Forty-six per cent of the voting electorate had supported Trump a few months before. Therefore this result implies that well under half of even those who voted for him did not believe in his defining policy proposal. The most plausible interpretation of this finding is that voters understood the Mexican-funded wall as a symbol of a wider approach rather than a concrete (pardon the pun) promise. Trump's willingness to make such a promise conveyed a style of getting things done and a preparedness to offend and challenge erstwhile international allies. It also sent a very clear signal that he would put a high premium on immigration control, and affinity with the values of people wary of Latino immigrants. Voters who backed him were in many cases expressing their endorsement of this approach to governing and the values that it implied Trump would follow, rather than weighing up the merits of a specific policy. They never expected the wall commitment to be implemented in anything close to the promised form (entirely rationally, given the Mexican government's position).

Seeing policies as a way of signalling about values rather than as firm commitments changes the nature and purpose of political debate. One obvious implication is a rather worrying one: that it doesn't matter whether a policy promise is deliverable or indeed bears any relation at all to reality. Trump certainly doesn't seem to have suffered damage among his supporters for his failure to deliver the wall as promised. Following this logic, there seem to be few constraints on politicians promising anything at all in order to send the messages that they want about the values they stand for. We will look further at political rhetoric and narrative in later chapters of this book.

Another implication of a theory that sees policies as a signalling tool is that it further undermines the median voter theory. Parties treating policies as value signals may well not tend towards the ideological centre, as those following the theory have often claimed. Subtle differences between policies around the median are not unlikely to be effective in sending signals, especially given the low attention most people pay to politics as set out above. It is unrealistic to expect voters to differentiate the values base of parties with similar moderate policies: such a strategy may well lead to the common 'person-in-the-street' criticism of politicians, that 'they are all the same'. Instead, dramatic statements of radical intent will cut through and convey a much more powerful symbolic meaning. The risk associated with radicalism is that it cannot be implemented (as with Trump's Mexican-funded wall) but, as we have seen, implementation is not the point. Therefore it can be argued that politicians actually have the opposite incentives to those hypothesised by the median voter theory. They are competing for scarce attention devoted to politics, and for an opportunity to send clear signals about their values. Many people do not expect them to implement the promised policies anyway. These dynamics mean that more extreme and eye-catching strategies may well be successful.

Conclusion

Trump's wall is, of course, not the first example of an undeliverable promise that has not prevented a politician from being elected or re-elected. Such rhetorical promises have been part of electioneering since ancient times. The question is how far this matters. The evidence set out above on the extent to which the public believe that policy commitments will be delivered implies that they recognise many policies will not be. People understand that politicians promise things that cannot be done (whether through deliberate strategy or over-estimation of their ability to see things through) and make their decisions accordingly. So a more honest political discourse is not just about being honest about the deliverability of promises. It is also about recognising the real role that such promises play, as symbols of values and a way of getting across an overall approach to governing. Seeing policies in this way has significant implications for how accountability works in democratic systems and for the ways in which we talk about policy and politics. These implications are addressed in detail in the next chapter.

7

Accountability in
a values-driven system

Policies may not be decisive in driving how voters make choices, but policies still matter. Every day, millions of people are affected by the level of tax, the operation of the health system or the rules for allocating welfare benefits. Policies have long-term macro impacts that shape the destiny of whole countries: the divided Germany example discussed in Chapter 5 was a particularly dramatic case. Whether a country has effective or ineffective policies is clearly important. One of the advantages that democracy is meant to have over other types of political system is that it seems to provide a direct route to accountability for bad policies, and therefore as a system it should tend to better ones. This chapter looks at the implications of putting culture and values at the heart of understanding the political system for how we think about accountability. It concludes that accountability is frequently ineffective, and suggests some different ways to try to deliver it that fit better with the implications of a focus on culture and values.

Elections and accountability

Basic democratic theory (what Achen and Bartels, 2016, call the 'folk theory') holds that elections provide accountability. Politicians who govern badly will be defeated at the ballot box. Therefore the democratic system provides clear incentives to come up with policies that work and that increase the welfare of citizens. Scrutiny by the press and by legislative institutions such as Parliament and Congress ensure that people can see whether policies are working and therefore make their decision in an informed way.

We have already seen, from the arguments in the last chapter, that accountability for individual policies is very unlikely to work in this way. Public understanding of politics and policy is simply too low and it would not be rational for voters to attempt to become more informed. Voters don't generally know whether or not a policy has worked (whatever 'worked' is deemed to mean in the context) and so they can't hold politicians to account appropriately. There may be another option, however, which would make lower demands on the cognitive capacity of the citizenry. This alternative is to say that people don't vote on specific policies, but on a much more general sense of whether the government is making them better off or not. In this version, people do not need to have a view on specific changes to regulations, tax or the design of public services. Instead, they can make a general judgement about their welfare and accord praise or blame to their political leaders accordingly. Accountability would therefore still be in place for government policy: if the sum of individual policies was negative for welfare, the responsible administration would suffer the consequences. If this is correct, even if the voters don't know or care about each policy the government has to, in case too many poor judgements tip the overall effect on voter welfare in the wrong direction.

For this argument to work, voters would need to be able to assess changes in their own welfare with reasonable accuracy and also make some sort of crude judgement about the extent to which the government was responsible. Without both of these factors being present, any accountability would be little better than random. Unfortunately for basic democratic theory, the evidence is against both of the requirements.

Taking these factors in reverse order, we can look first at whether voters show any ability to judge whether or not the government is responsible for changes in their welfare. Turning once again to Achen and Bartels (2016), they carried out some detailed analysis of presidential elections in the United States. The most striking piece is their work on the impact of shark attacks on the 1916 election. In July of that year, a series of shark attacks killed a number of swimmers at resorts on the Atlantic coast of New Jersey. Deadly shark attacks that far north at the height of the summer holiday season were unprecedented and caused near panic. What makes this case interesting for looking at whether voters are any good at attributing responsibility for changes in welfare is the fact that shark attacks affected some New Jersey counties but not all. In particular if a county was away from the beach (and therefore not susceptible to fear of sharks and reduced income from tourism as a result) it would act as a comparison. Therefore it was possible for Achen and Bartels to compare counties similar in demography, prior voting patterns and indeed all respects apart from vulnerability to shark attacks, and look at the impact on support for the incumbent president (Woodrow Wilson) at the election. Having cut the data in different ways and controlled for other factors as far as possible, they conclude that 'the horrifying shark attacks during the summer of 1916 reduced Wilson's vote in the beach communities by about ten percentage points' (Achen and Bartels, 2016: 126–7). As they go on to say, 'The government was helpless. But the voters punished anyway'.

The shark attacks case is a striking example of a tendency to hold governments 'accountable' for something they can do nothing about. Achen and Bartels then extend their analysis by looking at the impact of natural phenomena like floods and drought on voting in other presidential elections. They find widespread evidence for a negative impact on incumbent's vote share whenever such events have a major local impact, for example because an agricultural community suffers crop losses. They also find no evidence that the vote impact varies depending on the effectiveness of the government's response to the disaster. Incumbents are punished because voters feel fed up, regardless of whether the causes of that distress or its relative amelioration are anything to do with them. This kind of analysis raises major questions about whether elections are an effective tool for delivering accountability.

Facts and values

The other factor identified above as important for elections to provide accountability for general increases or decreases in welfare was that voters need to be capable of assessing changes in their welfare. This seems a reasonable assertion: don't people know if they are better off or not, or if their neighbours and colleagues are? Once we dive deeper, however, things start to look rather more complicated. People do not neutrally assess facts and then decide how they feel as a result. The phenomenon of confirmation bias kicks in. Confirmation bias is the psychological feature common to all of us, whereby we give additional weight to information that confirms our prior assumptions. Anyone who watches live sport will be familiar with this: fans are convinced that the referee should allow a score or give a penalty when their team would be the beneficiary, equally fervently believing the opposite if the decision would aid their opponents.

Confirmation bias works in politics as well, and connects back to our previous discussion of voting being driven by values. Chapter 6 implied that we frequently decide who to vote for based on a feeling for which candidate best reflects our fundamental values. This takes place on an emotional level, similar to how an ardent fan develops a connection to their sports team. We then interpret factual information in a way that best suits that prior connection. In the last chapter we looked at how values and cultural fit played a strong role in driving support for Donald Trump in 2016. That election also illustrates the dramatic way in which those emotional values-based connections can drive how we interpret facts, including those related to our own economic welfare. During the six months following Trump's election economic indicators in the United States were reasonably stable, continuing a period of steady growth and strong employment from the latter phase of Barack Obama's term in office. However perceptions of economic performance bore little relation to that stable picture. One set of data (Marquette, 2017) found that among Republican voters there was a net positive swing of 82 percentage points in their assessment of how the economy was doing in the six months after Trump's election. By this point Trump had not had time to carry out any significant economic policies. So not only were the objective indicators not pointing to radical economic improvement, there were also no policies in place that should create changed expectations. Instead the fact that their 'team' was in charge was enough to shift the Republican voters into feeling things were genuinely going better. Such a dynamic makes it hard to see how accountability for actual economic performance is going to work.

Confirmation bias is likely to be strongest on issues about which we feel the most deeply. These are likely to be where they fit most tightly with fundamental values. A recent piece of research tested how people react to and assess data depending on what issue it refers to (Sumner et al, 2018). The researchers presented people with statistical information of identical levels of complexity, but pertaining to different issues. One set of information referred to something value neutral (the effectiveness of a hypothetical new skin cream). The other set addressed immigration. There was a significant difference in people's ability to understand the information correctly, with accuracy decreasing markedly in the case of immigration. The strong prior values that many people hold about immigration issues impaired their ability to understand the data. This finding replicated that in a previous study in the United States which used gun control rather than immigration as the values-charged option (Kahan et al, 2017). Therefore it seems that values affect our ability to understand even basic information about how a policy works and about our own wellbeing. The causal link runs from values to assessment of facts, not the other way around.

Accountability failures

The implication of this conclusion is that accountability for policy decisions in a democratic system is often weak. Voters who feel a leader has the right values will support them, regardless of a high degree of policy failure. Partisan voters will downplay or ignore any objective indicators of policy failure, instead believing that success is just around the corner or is being unreasonably thwarted by political opponents. Politicians therefore have considerable leeway to implement risky or even disastrous policies if they retain partisan support that is driven by factors much more fundamental than policy, such as strong alignment on values.

There are plenty of examples that illustrate this point about the lack of accountability for failed policies. When I was working in the UK Ministry of Justice in 2014, the department's biggest priority was making radical changes to the probation service in England and Wales. The service was divided into two parts, with responsibility for overseeing the most serious criminals retained in the public sector and the other activity being outsourced to private companies operating in different regions of the country. These private contractors would be incentivised to cut costs and also to improve the high rates of reoffending by released criminals. This programme was complex, ambitious and driven at great speed, in part because of a political imperative to have it completed before the next general election due in 2015.

The programme, known as 'Transforming Rehabilitation' has now come to an end. In May 2019 the Ministry of Justice, under its fourth different Secretary of State since the reforms began, announced that the whole probation service would be brought back in house, ending the outsourcing experiment.[1] This volte-face came about as a result of intense criticism from many quarters of the performance of the reformed service. The Chief Inspector of Probation described the reformed model as 'irredeemably flawed'. The NAO, the official scrutiny body responsible to the UK Parliament, produced a report that was astonishingly direct given the usual careful measured style of government auditors. The NAO (2019: 1) said that 'The Ministry set itself up to fail in how it approached the Transforming Rehabilitation reforms'. It noted that despite the aim of incentivising measures to reduce reoffending 'the number of reoffences they [people who commit further offences] commit has increased significantly' and that the Ministry would need to pay out at least £467 million more than was required under the original contracts.

This NAO report and the response could be seen, in one sense, as an accountability mechanism working. The policy was scrutinised, found wanting and reformed. But the key point here is that there were no political consequences. The Secretary of State who had driven the programme through remained in the Cabinet, in a different post. Members of Parliament responded along party lines and supported their ministerial colleagues accordingly. And voters were almost certainly in the main entirely oblivious to the whole affair, despite the large amount of public money involved.

It is true that we should not expect voters to be especially interested in the probation service, as the vast majority will never come in contact with it. However, other examples show that there are also no political consequences for major policy failures in areas where a large number of people are direct service users. The London Underground carries 5 million passengers a day. Its visibility and potential political importance are probably disproportionately higher still given its location in the nation's capital and use by members of the media and people involved in the political process. In the mid-2000s the Labour government introduced a programme to change the way maintenance and upgrades of the network were managed, through a public–private partnership or 'PPP'. This programme led to a NAO report almost the equal in tone and damming content to the probation outsourcing example (NAO, 2009). It said that the programme caused the taxpayer direct losses of between £170 and £410 million, and also had a direct impact on passengers as improvements failed to be delivered. Crewe and King (2013) give a detailed account of the tube PPP failure. They argue that from the start it was almost certainly 'doomed' and that the total bill for the failure of the whole programme was not less than £2.5 billion.

Again, though, there were no serious political consequences. The London Underground programme was driven by the Treasury under Gordon Brown, and particularly his close adviser Shriti Vadera. She was subsequently promoted to a senior ministerial position. Although the failure was covered in the media, especially in London, there was no evidence of a public response to what happened. So again it is clear that the ways policy interacts with voting, and the ways that culture drives partisan support and which facts people take on board, act against effective accountability for bad policy.

The challenge to accountability goes deeper than the political level. Civil servants in the British system are, in theory, directly accountable to Parliament for the expenditure of public money. However my experience in the civil service was that in practice the imperative to deliver results on political timelines acts as a counter-weight to concerns about parliamentary scrutiny. I received a vivid illustration of the reality of accountability in the civil service for policy failure in one of the first projects I did as a graduate trainee in the Cabinet Office.

In 1999 there had been a run of difficulties with high-profile government technology projects. This came to a head when problems with a new computer system in the Passport Office led to huge backlogs just at the busiest time of year when people were preparing for their summer holidays. The Cabinet Office set up a team to review the series of failures and make recommendations for change. I was brought in as a junior team member to help with project management and organising the evidence that we would review.

One of the most significant failures we looked at (although much less public than the passports example) was in the immigration service. A new IT system for managing the flow of immigration cases had been disastrous. I remember interviewing the senior official brought in to sort out the mess afterwards in his office high up in a grim concrete tower block in a London suburb. He told me stories of how some staff, overwhelmed by the chaos caused by the new system, resorted to hiding files in cupboards or in one case tipping a whole load of them down a lift shaft. It became clear as we investigated that the premise of the new system was flawed, relying as it did on previously untested technology introduced at pace on a large scale. Back in my own office in Westminster, I dug out from the files the submission that had obtained the final sign-off to go ahead with this disastrous scheme. In the style of formal government approvals at that time it had a list of the senior officials involved on the top right hand side in descending order of seniority, with a note of when each of them had approved the project to go to the next stage. I remember looking at the names and wondering what the consequences had been for the people who signed off on this flawed scheme. One was by then one of the most senior civil servants in the whole of government. Another had been promoted to a high-profile post in the Cabinet Office, and a third now had a more senior role overseeing IT projects for other departments. This was my first insight into how accountability, or lack of it, fed down to the officials responsible for delivery. Ministers had been desperate for improved efficiency to reduce backlogs in the immigration system, and so the overwhelming imperative for these officials had been to press on with the scheme that on paper offered the opportunity to achieve that. When it failed they were seen to have done what was wanted.

Improving accountability

So far this chapter could feel like something of a council of despair. Not only do voters not understand detailed policy, they also don't seem to understand (or care) whether governments act to improve their general welfare. They vote on the basis of a general sense of how things are going, whether or not the government is responsible. More importantly, that sense of how things are going is grounded less in objective facts than in prior affinity with the culture and values expressed by the politicians how are in charge at any given time. Therefore it is not surprising that major policy failures occur on a regular basis, with seemingly few meaningful consequences for the politicians or officials involved. The rest of this chapter attempts to take a more optimistic note, by suggesting three ways we could re-think accountability to better accommodate culture and values.

Scrutinising culture and values

If voters are making their decisions on the basis of culture and values, a good starting point would be to focus more on those aspects in media coverage of politicians and their policy announcements. Debate and scrutiny of politics could make this a more significant feature. My experience is as a policy maker and policy analyst rather than an interviewer or journalist. Therefore I hope others with a greater track record in those fields take up the challenge of working out in more detail how to test and make explicit culture and values in discussions about policy. It seems to me that a good place to start would be to ask questions that put values at the centre. When a politician announces a new policy, it would be possible to test the values and cultural assumptions that sit behind it.

Why is the outcome that the policy aims to produce a good thing? Who will benefit from the policy and (crucially) what is the idea of justice or fairness that means those are the right beneficiaries? What does this policy say about our vision of the good society? Such questions immediately place values at the forefront of political debate.

Given the discussion above about what values are and where they come from it would be naive to think that anyone would be likely to change their view of a policy or a political leader as a result of such questioning. But at least we would be having an explicit conversation about the factors that actually determine how people will make their political choices. Current scrutiny is often focused on the costs of a policy, the practicalities of implementation or its place in a campaign strategy. The problems identified with the way accountability works mean that it is highly unlikely that these lines of questioning would change anyone's vote either. A politician who understands voter motivation will, in any case, answer questions around costs and practicalities not with the most accurate answer but with the one best calculated to send the desired signal about the culture and values they represent. Therefore a conversation about those factors themselves may be more direct, more honest and more useful.

Measuring culture and values

As Chapter 5 set out, governments do affect culture and values. Sometimes this is an explicit policy goal, at other times the effect is indirect and may not have been intended at all. Therefore one option for improving accountability is to make an effort to assess the extent to which policies do affect culture and whether that takes place in the intended way. Of course most voters will probably ignore a worthy assessment of whether a policy affects culture in the same way that they ignore an NAO report pointing out that the government has just wasted hundreds of millions on a failed policy. Looking at whether a policy has affected culture would not solve the problem of accountability for policy failure. What it would do, however, is contribute in another way to a more explicit and honest conversation about the role of policy being about cultural signalling as much as practical effect. We would at least be evaluating what a policy is actually doing. Such an assessment would also enable policy makers themselves to learn more about what works from this perspective of influencing culture. Given that they cannot help but have that influence, it is valuable to develop a better idea of how to do so.

There have not been, as far as I can find out, many serious attempts to analyse whether a policy that was intended to have an impact on culture and values has actually done so. However, it is possible to work out how such work could be done. A good example of a large scale change programme that was explicitly and publicly intended to have an impact on culture was the United Kingdom's privatisation programme in the 1980s and 1990s. The programme had several aims, some of which were narrower and not about culture change (for example, increasing access to investment capital and creating efficiency through competition). However, government communications at the time were clear that there was a wider culture change goal. Ministers from Prime Minister Margaret Thatcher downwards wished to spread acceptance of share ownership and a wider sense of a stake in the capitalist system (Myddelton, 2014; Heald, 1988).

An evaluation of this programme therefore ought to have looked at this cultural aspect as well as the economic factors which have in practice dominated assessments of privatisation (for example, Helm and Jenkinson, 1997). It would be interesting to see whether attitudes to private capital and entrepreneurship changed more among those who received shares than among the general population, or among those who worked within the industries directly affected. Potential changes to values and attitudes could be measured with good survey data. For example, the British Social Attitudes survey already includes questions about people's attitudes to state provision of welfare services.[2] The Conservative ministers responsible for implementing the privatisation programme would have hoped to see a shift in these values towards more private provision as a result of the changes they introduced. This kind of question potentially runs up against the issue identified in Chapter 1 whereby the attitudes people express may not line up well with what they actually do. Therefore an attempt to assess the impact on culture of privatisation would need to look at behaviours that could act as proxies for the underlying attitudes. Examples that could have been used for this could be the rates of self-employment or examples of starting new businesses in the relevant group. The British Social Attitudes survey also contains the necessary information to do such analysis.

The privatisation example is just an illustration of the kind of work that could give better insights into whether the impact of a policy on culture and values was as intended. Much more detailed methodological work would be needed to create a robust test for a particular policy. That feels like an area of work worth developing for the analytical teams within government departments and the academic teams outside with whom they work. As I have suggested elsewhere (Muers, 2019), maybe government departments need to augment their Chief Economists with Chief Anthropologists, who specialise in understanding culture.

Front-line feedback

So far in this chapter we have been discussing accountability as it applies to policy makers in government. However, as Chapter 2 demonstrated, those are not the most important actors when it comes to the reality of policy implementation. Our 'street-level bureaucrats' – teachers, nurses, police officers and social workers – are the ones whose actions affect citizens directly. Given a choice, I suspect many voters would say that their priority would be their family doctor feeling direct responsibility and accountability for providing a good service. This would be more important to them than the Secretary of State for Health facing consequences if the national health budget as a whole was overspent. Therefore, one way to make accountability more effective is to make it more tailored to the mission of service improvement at the front-line. This route to improvement is a more direct one, via immediate changes in practice rather than political pressure on decision makers to change course.

The kind of evaluation discussed in the policy failure examples above is probably not what is needed for this purpose. While I am sure that many employees of the London Underground felt angry about the waste of money associated with the PPP process, the many detailed accounts of how and why it failed would have done nothing to help them deliver a better service for the public. In my time in government I was involved in commissioning and or reviewing many policy studies. Most of them aimed to answer fundamental questions about the impact of the policy over several years. While often of very high quality, these studies have limited practical utility for service practitioners. An important reason for that is the time they take to produce. By the time the study concludes whether or not the policy was a good idea, not only has the political spotlight moved elsewhere but the reality on the ground has also shifted in response to technology, social change or resource pressures. The lessons we learnt from these studies were often very helpful for the delivery system as it was a year before, rather than today. Rather sadly, these high-quality and often quite expensive research findings are put out into the public domain with the minimum of fanfare and quickly forgotten. The final day of the Parliamentary term before summer recess, when media attention is elsewhere and there is a deluge of business from across government, is a favourite date for the publication of no-longer-relevant research reports.[3]

Speed of feedback, then, is critical if front-line public sector workers are to be accountable to the citizens they work with and able to learn and respond to what happens. Modern technology makes immediate user-friendly feedback much easier to collect and deliver. Private sector service delivery companies clearly understand this: yesterday I checked out of a hotel and within an hour received an email asking a few simple questions about my stay and the quality of the customer service. Some public sector organisations have been using these kinds of rapid feedback mechanisms for a while. There was a phase in the early 2000s when policy makers in the United Kingdom were obsessed by Compstat, the near-real-time information and performance management approach used by the New York City Police. This may or may not have been in part because of the starring role taken by the Baltimore version of the system in Season Three of the hit television series 'The Wire'. I remember Compstat coming up repeatedly in discussions in the Cabinet Office about UK public services and whether we could implement something similar.

Compstat had some strong top-down elements, in that the information was partly used by senior management to put pressure onto local leaders to improve performance. An alternative model is to focus more on accountability out to citizens rather than upwards to management, which is more in keeping with the overall goal addressed in this chapter. In an extremely simple example, my local council (and I assume many others) allows immediate electronic notification of a missed rubbish collection. Not only can they then arrange a replacement collection but by looking at patterns of such reports it is possible for them and the contractors running the service to tweak the schedules for the collection teams in order to mitigate potential problems. A more sophisticated version of this is the BOS:311 app used in Boston, which enables citizens to report a wide range of minor problems and to receive updates on progress with how the city authorities are attempting to resolve them (Jordan, 2019).

A much larger and more complex example in the United Kingdom is the Friends and Family Test in the National Health Service. It simply asks a patient whether they would recommend the service they have received to a friend or family member. In August 2019 the system was collecting around 1.2 million pieces of feedback every month.[4] The purpose of the test is to give clinicians and managers information that they can use to improve their services, and at the time of writing (summer 2019) the NHS was carrying out a review of the test to ensure that it was best designed to suit that goal. At a more global level, the World Bank has recognised that new technology opens up ways for all governments, including in developing countries, to connect directly with citizens and receive their feedback on service delivery.[5] Nesta (2019b) looked at international examples of how public services used data in imaginative ways, and concluded that one of the main benefits was that 'frontline teams and organisations can optimise their way of working, making more informed and impactful decisions at the same time' (2019b: 10). All of these examples demonstrate that simple and widely available technology can easily make accountability rapid and responsive. The data can be used by senior management and politicians in a more command and control environment, by teams among themselves to improve their practice or by citizens to see what is going on and respond to it. A new model of accountability is already developing, which is more likely to lead to service improvements than a version that depends on creating pressure on senior level decision makers through the political system.

Conclusion

Repeated policy failure, and the lack of consequences for the decision makers responsible, implies that current systems of accountability are not up to the task. This is not surprising, as voters do not make decisions based on whether a policy is a success or even whether they are generally better off as a result of a government's overall programme. Instead deep-seated political attachments based on cultural alignment drive how people interpret policy success and whether their welfare has improved. In this context, there are three ways to improve accountability. First, the values and cultural norms being signalled by policies should be raised in debate and scrutinised. Second, whether or not policies have succeeded in affecting culture and values in the way intended should be analysed and discussed. Third, if one of the aims of accountability is to improve outcomes for citizens then rapid real-time feedback mechanisms, used by front-line workers rather than policy makers, are likely to be more effective than traditional policy evaluation. The balance of resources could shift from the latter to the former, building on the many interesting examples that are already in place around the world.

PART THREE

How policy makers can take culture seriously

In Parts One and Two, I set out why culture and values are important to policy makers, firstly because of the direct impact they have and secondly because of how they affect the political context. At the end of the last chapter I set out some ideas for how we could change approaches to accountability in a way that takes culture and values as seriously to the extent I believe is necessary. Part Three continues this work of suggesting different approaches and solutions that policy makers can employ in response to the issues raised in the first two parts.

Adapting policy-making practice to the importance of culture and values is not easy. It requires different mindsets and some new approaches. As I will set out, most of those new approaches have roots in experiments or practices that are already underway or being tried somewhere. However in most cases they are not sufficiently mainstream that there is a strong body of evidence in place to demonstrate their effectiveness. Therefore Part Three of this book is more speculative and is rooted strongly in examples from my own experience and from other individual cases, and less in an established body of academic literature. My hope is that the ideas here inspire other practitioners to try things out and share what happens, and inspire researchers to look into whether any of what I suggest really addresses the challenges raised by putting culture and value at the centre of our understanding of public policy. Each of the four chapters in this part looks at one strategy for addressing culture and values: taking symbols seriously, doing more locally, building organisations and being smart about evidence.

8

Taking symbols seriously

Chapter 5 argued that policies often play a symbolic rather than a practical role. They can be intended as symbols of a government's value-set and cultural identification rather than commitments to be implemented faithfully. Voters often interpret them in this light as well, and react to political leaders' policy promises accordingly. If this reading of the role of policy is even partly right, then policy makers need to take the symbolic role of policy seriously. This means that they need to apply professional skill and understanding to this aspect of policy as much as to any other.

Should we care about symbols?

In my experience the policy-making system is some way from this level of seriousness about policies as symbols. I have on several occasions heard a policy called 'symbolic' in a way that is meant as an insult: implying that it is somehow not a real or serious policy but a short-term gimmick. When I was responsible for coordinating the UK government's legislative programme I spent a lot of time working with the Parliamentary Counsel. These are the specialist lawyers who literally write the law: crafting the words that Parliament considers to put the intention of ministers into statute. I remember conversations with members of the Office of Parliamentary Counsel becoming very pained when ministers wanted to include symbolic elements in legislation. The political logic in play here was that including in a law a statement of what the government wanted to be the case was a way of sending a message, especially if political opponents could be made to vote against it because of their disagreements with other substantive elements of the draft law. However, the Counsel frequently couldn't get their heads around this. Their job was to convey policy into clear and precise language with unambiguous legal effect. If the only effect intended was to send a message, then that was in their eyes not a legal concept and should be left to the communications department.

I had, and still have, considerable sympathy with this view from the Parliamentary Counsel. Legal text that would only ever be seen by Members of Parliament and a few external specialists always seemed to me to be a pretty strange vehicle for trying to send a message about a government's intentions. However, the wider view of which it is a symptom, that the potential symbolic effects of policy are less important, needs closer scrutiny.

The relative lack of attention given to symbolic power by policy makers may be linked to the state of development of the relevant theory in academic discussions. In his comprehensive review of the public policy literature, Parsons (2001: 178) argues that 'the study of such issues [symbols] has not, until comparatively recently, been central to the study of the policy process'. He goes on to reflect that deeds and rationality have been more central to academic theory about how policy is made than words, rhetoric and symbols.

The strongest theoretical basis for understanding the role of symbols in policy comes from the work of Murray Edelman. He argues that the real power in policy making lies in the way symbols are used and manipulated to construct understandings of both problems and solutions (Edelman, 1988). In his view symbols come in two types. The first are what he calls 'referential', in that they refer to some real resources that are being distributed by the policy concerned. The second he terms 'condensational' or emotional symbols that reassure people and give an illusion that action is being taken, regardless of whether it is or not. He believes referential symbols to be limited in number, given the inevitable lack of real resources that any government will face. Therefore much political and policy-making activity becomes focused on the emotional type, where resource constraints bite to a much lesser extent. He believes that citizens therefore face not a world of facts and policies that respond to them but a 'spectacle' of 'constructed problems' (Edelman, 1988: 1).

In the title of another of his works (1977) Edelman coined the phrase 'words that succeed and policies that fail'. By this he meant that a policy may succeed as a rhetorical or symbolic device but fail to address the problem at which it is notionally targeted. I find the concept of 'failure' being used here interesting: if the policy is intended to be symbolic, and citizens react to it on that level, is the lack of a real-world impact actually a failure? Surely if people respond to the words and the symbol as intended, the policy maker could count that as a success? The implication of Edelman's title is that there is still an objective goal out there that the policy 'ought' in some sense to be affecting. On the evidence discussed in the previous chapters, it is perhaps more likely that everyone concerned is acting on the basis that there is not.

Examples of taking symbols seriously

Edelman's work, and that of others following his lead, shows how symbolic action is at the heart of policy making. Young and Mason (1983) argue that the general public may be ahead of the policy professionals who are wary of talking about symbols. They believe 'the intelligent citizen has long been aware that a large part of government action is symbolic rather than substantive' (1983: 216). It is straightforward to find examples of government actions that are explicitly symbolic and for which there is no supposed 'real' impact beyond the symbolism.

One such example is where governments take a strong interest in statues and other relics of history, in an attempt to construct a certain cultural national narrative. A few years ago I visited Sofia, the capital of Bulgaria. My most striking memory of that trip is from visiting a patch of grass next to a housing estate somewhere on the outskirts of the city. There, in various stages of disrepair, was a large collection of statues from Bulgaria's time as part of the Soviet bloc. Giant stone Lenins with their fists raised sit alongside likenesses of forgotten members of the Bulgarian Communist leadership and (most disturbing to me) a severe bust of Felix Dzerzhinsky, founder of the KGB. Placing all these icons of the past in such an unprepossessing location, like so many oversized garden gnomes, is a very clear symbol of the cultural change desired by a new governing class once the Communist regime had been overthrown.

Studies of other countries in the former Soviet bloc have also shown the power of policy around history and statues and the symbolic resonance that these issues can create. Burch and Smith (2008) looked at the case of Estonia, and what they termed a 'war of monuments'. They show how Estonia's troubled 20th-century history made the symbolism of monuments to military campaigns extremely emotive. The Estonian government took this symbolic issue seriously enough to pass a law in 2007 giving it new powers over the location and nature of monuments. Its subsequent use of that power (to move a Soviet-era memorial away from the centre of Tallinn, the Estonian capital) led to 'large-scale riots' (Burch and Smith, 2008: 915). In the context of a small new nation trying to find an identity between Russia and the European Union, and with a large Russian-speaking minority population, policy makers have no choice but to engage with how to manage symbols as effectively as possible. Their skill in doing so has implications for public security and the survival of governments.

Skills and capabilities for symbolic policy

Those skills that policy makers in Estonia and Bulgaria had to develop are also needed by their counterparts in other countries. There is nothing new to arguing that a grasp of how narrative and symbols work is an essential part of the toolkit of a public servant. In the ancient world, rhetoric was at the core of the curriculum for any aspiring statesman. Ceremony was also extremely important: the most powerful policy makers of the Roman Republic had to carry out elaborate religious rituals around any significant public events, with mistakes leading to the whole procedure being repeated or even an important moment such as the election of a new Consul being cancelled.

Modern policy makers do not, thankfully, need to learn as much about the symbolic meaning of animal entrails as their ancestors in Ancient Rome. However, they do need to understand more about symbols, language and messages than is currently often the case. This understanding needs to go beyond a superficial awareness that messaging and symbolism matters, especially because political leaders are often interested in it. One characteristic of an effective political leader is an ability to communicate their political goals as simple stories that resonate with an often disinterested populace. Symbolic action and simple words that act almost as homilies can be remarkably effective. For example, after the 2008 financial crash, the Conservative party explained their economic policy as 'fixing the roof':[1] a compelling image rather removed from the reality of public spending reduction. Richards (2019) uses examples across recent British history to draw out how good leaders often act as 'political teachers' who use symbols and stories to build support.

If teaching and storytelling is so important to political leaders, those who advise them need professional tools and structured ways of thinking about these issues. In my experience of Masters of Public Policy courses and similar education programmes, there is a heavy focus on law and economics, with a little social research and political science. There is generally much less content that gives people grounding in the reality of managing symbols. Some signs of progress towards this are emerging. Stanford University recently launched a 'Statement on Education for Public Problem Solving' which calls for a different approach to educating policy makers. It argues that traditional social scientific tools are not enough, and policy makers need grounding in 'the craft or practice of solving public problems, focusing on the ability to formulate tractable problems, understand the interests of key stakeholders, organize coalitions for change, communicate objectives'.[2] This broader approach may, if it takes root, contain some of the change that we need.

To bring this suggestion about different capabilities to life, I can take the example of my former role in charge of sentencing policy in the Ministry of Justice in London. Discussions with ministers about policy often involved a political desire to 'send a message' on some types of crime by toughening sentencing.

Knife-related violence was a particular political focus during my period in the role. There were two audiences of interest in this case: worried citizens who needed reassurance; or potential criminals whom the minister wished to deter. If we were really honest, none of those involved (the minister, his political advisors or me as the senior civil servant) really knew what message or symbolic action would be effective with those specific groups. These discussions felt like a classic example of decision making on the basis of anecdote and assumption. Often we ended up taking the views of a few particular media outlets as a proxy for the wider public. More seriously, we were guilty of assuming that the people who might be involved in knife crime would respond to messages and signals in a similar way to us, who had very little in common with them in terms of background and understanding. The policy was intended to send a message (and was often explicitly described in such terms). Being really effective at sending a message would have required us to have the knowledge of the sub-cultures, narratives, problem framing and symbols used by those we were aiming it at. We were certainly not at this level of professional capability. Personally I have come across few public organisations that are, although I hope there are good examples I have not discovered.

The lack of training to help policy makers understand how symbols work and how to create narratives that intersect with the cultures they are working with reflects a deeper problem: policy-making practice tends to take too narrow a view of human motivation. Government policy processes often place cost-benefit analysis at the centre, with the consequence that financially-quantifiable issues are prioritised. The Impact Assessments that are required to accompany all major new policies in the United Kingdom similarly focus on economic issues, or the economic impact of wider concerns like environmental sustainability. I have never seen an Impact Assessment that makes a serious attempt to grapple with the impact on culture that a policy might have, whether an alternative would be better and whether that impact is coherent with other policies that might be underway.

One of the largest tasks faced by any government in the developed world is designing and managing a system of social welfare benefits. This is an area where economic analysis rubs up sharply against other ways of looking at the world. Gray and Timmins (2018) studied 30 years of attempts to update and improve the British system of social security for people of working age (essentially those aged 18–65). They found that the responsible department, the Department for Work and Pensions, took great pride in the quality of its economic analysis, had access to sophisticated datasets and even the officials without formal analytical training were comfortable handling quantitative information. This was all to be commended. However, they also found that the department was much weaker on 'ethnographic and anthropological data that might help the department to understand the lives of the people it was trying to help' (Gray and Timmins, 2018: 4). This reliance on economic data rather than understanding of the wider meanings that a policy might have for the citizens affected led to approaches that failed and needed to be revised. Gray and Timmins cite the example of reforms affecting Carers Allowance, which failed to take account of the symbolic value to the recipient of even a very small amount of money that was controlled independently of someone else who was the main household earner. This policy symbolised much more to the people affected than an economic analysis was capable of demonstrating, and therefore attempts to change it rapidly ran into unforeseen opposition.

Managing new skills and capabilities

So policy makers will be more effective if they are allowed, in their own organisational cultures, to take symbols and narrative seriously and if they are properly trained in tools and techniques for doing so. There is an obvious challenge to this latter point. If governments increase their professional capabilities in framing problems, taking symbolic actions and managing narrative, they may not use this for desirable ends. A skilled storyteller can drift into being a skilled liar, and understanding how to construct symbols is barely a shade away from being manipulative. If we think of people in history in positions of political power who have demonstrated great abilities in these fields, some dangerous and unpleasant characters (think of Robespierre or Goebbels) come high up the list.

Misuse of these new capabilities is undoubtedly a risk. One response is to develop a new system of professional ethics alongside new professional skills. In the United Kingdom at least, existing groups of professionals in government have accepted codes of practice with strong cultural force for the group's members. For example the statisticians have a clear process and set of practices to avoid political manipulation of official data, as well as an independent statistical authority to oversee the whole process. Government scientists adhere to protocols around peer review and how data is published. Designing the appropriate codes and practices, which in turn will hopefully develop a healthy culture, for those who become experts in the role of government as a creator of symbols is beyond both the scope of this book and my own expertise. I offer it as a challenge to interested and qualified readers.

Another response to the challenge is to consider the alternative. If policy makers do not develop better skills in working with the symbolic and cultural context they affect, they will not stop doing the work regardless. As we have seen, the very nature of policies is that they have symbolic force as least as much as direct impact, regardless of the intent of those working on them. Therefore if we do not develop the right capabilities to manage this force, out of fear that they will be misused, we will simply continue to do the work badly or as an accidental by-product of other policy making. Also, those who by nature or learning do become skilled at managing symbols will have a large systemic advantage, and there is no assurance that they will be benign in their use of it.

Conclusion

We need to move on from 'symbolic' being a term of derision in policy making. Instead we need to accept that many policies have a symbolic nature, whether or not that is explicitly their goal. The way politics interacts with culture and values makes this an inevitable feature of the policy landscape. There are examples of policy makers engaging directly in managing symbols (like the Estonian statues), examples of them trying to do so without the necessary tools (like in the sentencing case) and examples where the symbolic aspect and its impact on motivation and behaviour was underplayed (the social security example). Across the board, I believe our policy-making practice would be improved by a more serious effort at training in the importance of understanding symbols to good policy practice, in the tools and approaches that would help make sense of them, and the ethics and culture that need to underpin their use in a healthy society.

9

Doing more locally

Chapter 2 set out how central direction is less important than one might think from the attention that the media give to what central governments do in different policy fields. A centrally-determined strategy sets a context and direction, but is mediated through the culture of the local organisations that are charged with delivery. Chapter 6 looked at accountability, and identified that the way that culture and values interact with the political system means that accountability for central government policy decisions is often weak. This makes it all too easy for bad decisions and poor strategies to be pushed through with no consequences. One obvious conclusion to draw from these two findings is that it would be sensible to re-think the role of central decision making. If central decisions will generally not be implemented with any accuracy, and those making them will not be held accountable for the consequences, would it not be more effective to disperse and devolve power where possible and rely on more of the front-line direct accountability measures that outlined in Chapter 6?

The challenges of centralism

I received a stark lesson in how policy intentions from the centre collide with messy social reality in delivery when I was working for the Prime Minister's Strategy Unit. In 1993 the then Conservative government in the United Kingdom set up the Child Support Agency. This was a new government body charged with obtaining child maintenance payments from parents who were not living with their children. The idea was in part to provide more support for the parents who were taking day-to-day responsibility for childcare, but also to offset the cost to the government of providing welfare benefits, which was the alternative if child maintenance was not forthcoming. By the mid-2000s, when I became involved, the Agency had become a byword in UK government circles for poor performance, missed targets, computer problems and ministers constantly having to apologise to Members of Parliament for the appalling service that their constituents had suffered. I was asked to lead a team supporting an external independent review of the whole child support system, from the policy framework to the delivery approach.

My team and I wanted to understand what was going on and why there were so many problems. We spent a day at the Child Support Agency office in Plymouth, talking to staff and seeing how they operated and the challenges they faced. The experience that really brought home to me what the Agency was grappling with came when I sat with a woman who was a senior case manager in what was ominously called the 'complex cases team'. She dealt with the messy situations: where there were multiple children involved who had different parents, or a parent had erratic income from self-employment, or was in prison, or indeed several of this sort of complication at once. Of course human society being what it is, these 'complex cases' were far from unusual. This case manager and her colleagues were equipped with computer systems that carried all the rules of the child maintenance regime (who was entitled to what under what circumstances) and also the welfare benefits regime (including what child support money flowed to the individual and what flowed to the government to offset benefit payments). The idea was that you entered all the information of the particular situation and the computer calculated a maintenance figure as a result. The problem was that the central government civil servants who drew up the rules had not (and probably never could have) accounted for all the interactions of circumstances that actually existed. There were always combinations of factors that fell outside the rules, or were technically in the rules but created perverse outcomes. Therefore the computer system, based on those rules, couldn't cope with the complex cases and either gave out an unusable answer or failed completely.

The case manager I was with showed me that for the really complex examples she had to do the work by hand. She sketched out all the interactions and potential payments in the case on a large piece of paper, working out the financial flows on a calculator. She cared about the work and was determined to get a fair and just outcome. But each case took literally hours, while the work at the Agency overall mounted up. In 2006 there was a backlog of 923,000 cases that were stuck on an old computer system (NAO, 2006).

Two dynamics had created this situation, and with it terrible outcomes for both the people the Agency was aiming to help and for the frustrated staff who worked there. The first was that both the benefits system and the child maintenance system were extremely detailed frameworks of rules. There is always a trade-off in these kinds of social welfare allocation systems between an attempt to be fair to everyone in every situation and the complexity that such an approach creates. Ministers and civil servants in the United Kingdom had, with both of these systems, decided to attempt to specify rules for a huge number of situations to ensure they were clear and everyone was treated appropriately. Managing one such system when it meets the reality of how people live their lives was tricky. The Child Support Agency was attempting to implement the interface of two such systems of centrally-determined rules, both of which frequently changed as a result of political decisions. It was not surprising that both the computers and the staff could hardly cope.

The second dynamic was that the case manager I was observing, and her colleagues, felt they had no discretion or ability to make judgements about what was proportionate and sensible. In everyday life, humans respond to complexity and multiple imperatives by adopting rules of thumb or heuristics (Kahneman and Tversky, 1974). While these cognitive shortcuts can lead to diminished accuracy, they increase speed and enable us to respond to uncertainty and information overload. Risks to accuracy could hardly have been worse had the case managers been exercising intelligent judgement rather than working out maintenance payments with a flow-chart drawn on a piece of paper and a calculator. The system did not allow for judgement, however. Every conclusion had to be grounded in a detailed working through of the rules, whatever answer that produced and whether or not it equated to a lay-person's sense of natural justice. One of the problems the Agency encountered was that in complex and unusual cases the answer produced by the interactions of its rules and the benefit system sometimes seemed absurd. A good example was quoted in a Parliamentary debate about the performance of the child support system in November 2003: an order to deduct maintenance from someone's earnings to the tune of 1p.[1] It seemed to me that more local ability to make judgements and adapt to the circumstances that the case managers were facing would have improved the service and the outcomes.

My experience of the Child Support Agency is backed up by more systematic research. Researchers from the Centre for Public Impact have looked at a large number of case studies of different public policies across the world. When summarising all the lessons they had learnt from them, they too concluded that complex public services were not amenable to control from the top. The ability to develop bespoke solutions to individual local circumstances was too important. They also noted that the tools required to administer top-down systems ended up creating stress and poorer performance for the staff attempting to operate them, as I had found at the Child Support Agency in Plymouth. Instead they suggest sharing power between levels and actors in a system and enabling front-line workers and citizens to take more control (Bagnera and Gagliani, 2019).

Giving power to staff, like the complex cases manager I met, is one reason to have more local control. Another is to move power even further away from the centre, to the citizens themselves. Designing public services with the mindset of enabling individual citizens and communities to support themselves and one another can have powerful consequences. The potential of this shift in approach is powerfully demonstrated by Hilary Cottam's book *Radical Help* (2018). In it she sets out five experiments that she and her team designed to tackle social challenges in England. The experiments ranged across different policy areas:

health, employment, parenting, ageing and supporting young people. Despite this broad range, the principles underpinning all the experiments were similar. These included starting from the vision and the capabilities of the individuals involved, and building the service offer upwards from there regardless of previous rules and procedures within the delivery system concerned. All the experiments delivered impressive positive results for the beneficiaries.

Cottam's book also highlights one of the other dangers of centralism: it can by its nature kill off promising new approaches. She explains how in 2010 the then Prime Minister, David Cameron, came to visit one of her team's experiments: the Life programme in Swindon. Life was a new set of approaches for supporting vulnerable families. The Prime Minister was so impressed by the early results of the new service that he asked for it to be replicated nationally. Civil servants from central government came to see what could be done. Cottam then tells how the well-meaning attempt to build on her success was counter-productive. 'An approach based on … a shift in power to the families was translated into a linear programme with outputs that could be measured and controlled' (Cottam, 2018: 250). She concludes that ultimately she and her team 'faced a challenge we were not able to overcome: we could not persuade central government to think differently'. The very characteristics of the approach that enabled it to work were fundamentally incompatible with a national roll-out driven by central government. If Cottam is right to argue that in many cases an approach that is fundamentally grounded in individual and community experience is most likely to work, and the results of her work and other programmes like it imply that she may well be, there are large areas of social policy where central intervention will be inherently counter-productive.

The challenges to localism

If there are such clear advantages to giving local discretion and accountability in the management of complex public services, why does it not happen more often? This is a particularly pressing question in the United Kingdom, which is more centralised than most other developed Western countries,[2] but the same arguments are relevant elsewhere. Another project I was involved in during my time at the Prime Minister's Strategy Unit gave me some insights into the objections to localism. The project aimed to take an overall strategic look at the role of local government in England. We were responding to a general if rather vague sense that there was unrealised potential in the local government sector and that councils could achieve more and create a closer connection with their citizens if changes were made. The irony of a group of policy advisers in Admiralty Arch in central London doing this work was painfully obvious, so we tried with mixed success to open the process up to views from local leaders.

After some months of work we concluded that there were significant opportunities to strengthen the role of local government. We demonstrated that there was a clear link between the extent to which people thought local government was responsible for important decisions, and their propensity to turn out at elections: why vote if you are choosing someone who is only responsible for decisions that don't matter?[3] We also identified several areas where there were sound policy and governance reasons for devolving more power away from central government.

Despite the work and the supporting analysis, our recommendations found little traction in government. Other departments, as well as the Prime Minister's advisers in No 10 and the Treasury, were wary of ceding control and saw too many risks involved to launch into wholesale change. There were two main arguments they deployed against greater localism, which were not unique to the work I was involved in and continue to be used now.

The first argument is that local control leads to too much variation in the nature and quality of the services provided in different parts of the country. In the United Kingdom the pejorative short-hand for such an outcome is the 'postcode lottery': what service you receive being determined by where you live rather than by an objective assessment of need.[4] Such an outcome is presented as the antithesis of the principle of the National Health Service (in particular, although the term is also used with regard to other services): that need should be the overriding factor in determining who benefits from the service. The argument is that national service standards, funding regimes and performance management are needed to guard against such local variation, which is both unfair in principle and politically unacceptable.

The second argument against greater local control that we encountered related to the impact on the reputation of central government. The point, put forcefully to us by political advisers in particular, was that even if control for policy was devolved the politicians at national level would still get the blame when things went wrong. Someone who had suffered from a delayed hospital operation, a failure to catch the culprit for a burglary or repeated transport delays would not care who was notionally in charge. Through local Members of Parliament and the media these problems would still land on the desk of the minister for the relevant department in London. If they were to be blamed for problems, those ministers wanted some control and assurance that everything possible was being done to reduce the likelihood of them coming to pass. The fear was that political culture in the United Kingdom was such that the desire of citizens to punish government for failure, regardless of justification (as we saw in Chapter 7) tended to end up at the centre.

These two objections, along with the inevitable arguments about money, prevented most of the conclusions of our project coming to fruition at the time. The following sections look at the two objections – the postcode lottery and continued central accountability – in the light of the previous chapters and what a focus on culture and values tells us about how things actually work.

Responding to the challenges: the 'postcode lottery'

There is a critical assumption behind the postcode lottery argument, namely that central decision making and common service standards will lead to a consistent service offering to the public. If a centralised approach doesn't have this standardising effect, and the differences across postcodes exist regardless, then the argument against decentralisation falls away.

The discussion of 'street-level bureaucrats' in Chapter 2 set out a strong theoretical basis for scepticism about whether it is possible to avoid a postcode lottery, even in situations where services are controlled centrally. The potential points of variation and the ways in which culture in different front-line delivery institutions can affect results persist despite control mechanisms being imposed. So there is good reason to believe that the postcode lottery will continue even in situations of ostensible central control.

As noted above, in the United Kingdom the postcode lottery concept is particularly emotive when applied to the NHS. Successive governments have introduced national service standards and inspection regimes in an attempt to create a consistent quality of care in the different health providers across the country. Despite all this, the problems with achieving uniform delivery that the street-level bureaucrats theory predicts still remain. To begin demonstrating this with an example, when I was preparing to write this chapter I came across an account of the personal consequences of a postcode lottery within the NHS that brought it dramatically to life. Lorna Finlayson (2019) wrote in the *London Review of Books* about her brother's experience with a finger injury. His local hospital initially prescribed a course of antibiotics, which didn't resolve the problem. More antibiotics followed, with similar lack of results. Concerned about what was happening, he ended up going to the Accident and Emergency Department at the famous Addenbrooke's hospital in Cambridge, where a different medical team realised that the problem was much more serious, with the risk of developing into a potentially fatal infection of the bone, and took action accordingly.

Finlayson's article sets out just one case of where the locality a patient was in made a huge difference. It would also be possible to argue that the problem here could be too little central control rather than too much: for all the rhetoric, the NHS is not entirely centralised and local management teams and clinicians do have some discretion. Maybe tighter performance management of the local hospital in this case could have driven it to deliver at the level of Addenbrooke's? A more comprehensive study of an even more centralised service provides some countervailing evidence.

The NAO (2013) looked at performance of the Jobcentre Plus network. These are the offices around the United Kingdom that aim to support unemployed people back into work, and as such are part of a national system with one regime of benefits, sanctions and options to offer customers. The study found that even in this classic top-down bureaucracy there was major variation in practice. The caseload per adviser, identified as an important driver of performance, varied from an average of 213 in the highest region to 118 in the lowest. Even within local districts (that is, jobcentres located near one another and therefore more likely to be serving a similar population and economy) in some cases staffing levels varied by nearly 30 per cent (NAO, 2013: 20–21). So there is evidence to support the theoretical case that variation in service levels is effectively unavoidable. It may be possible to standardise the delivery of a simple product, but the people-focused services that governments are generally responsible for seem not to be amenable to uniformity. Therefore arguing against localism on the grounds that it would create a postcode lottery is not convincing. The lottery already exists and people are playing it every day, regardless of the amount of central control.

Responding to the challenges – central accountability

The other challenge, around whether blame falls on central government for mistakes even if decisions have been devolved, rests on two pillars. First, that the public do in fact lay blame in that way. Second, that it is a problem for central government if they do so.

Starting with the first point, this time the discussion in previous chapters actually reinforces the challenge to localism. In Chapter 5 I set out the limited extent to which voters understand policy and political institutions. In complex modern bureaucracies, with different funding streams, outsourcing and so on, it is hard even for a policy expert to stay on top of exactly which arm of government is responsible for what. Expecting members of the public to do so, with their busy lives and other interests, is thus pretty unreasonable. It would not, then, be surprising if the simplest shortcut for anyone aggrieved at an experience with government is to hold high-profile national politicians responsible for anything and everything.

National politicians certainly often act as if they feel the need to take responsibility for local failings. A famous recent example of this in the United Kingdom was the 'Baby P' case.[5] In 2007 a one-year-old baby, Peter Connelly, was found dead. His mother and his mother's partner were subsequently found guilty of causing his death. It emerged that local social services and health services had seen Peter several times but had missed clear warning signals that he had been harmed and was at serious risk. The responsible Secretary of State, Ed Balls, intervened personally in the case and required the Director of Social Services in the relevant London borough to be sacked and replaced by someone nominated by his department. This was despite child protection being a clear local responsibility, with legal accountability resting with the council concerned. The balance between central and national roles in this case generated major controversy, with the Secretary of State's actions ultimately ending up in front of the UK Supreme Court.

So it does seem that the public may, at least some of the time, lay the blame for local failings at the door of national politicians. This takes us on to the second point: does this matter? At this point, the discussion of culture and values in previous chapters points in a different direction. We established in Chapter 7 that voters do not really hold politicians to account for particular decisions or particular outcomes. Instead they interpret decisions and their consequences in the light of pre-existing assumptions and values. We saw how, as a result, direct responsibility for disastrous policies generally has few political consequences. If there are few consequences for bad decisions that someone actually makes, it seems a stretch to assert that there will be such consequences for decisions that were actually taken locally by somebody else.

Achen and Bartels' (2016) assessment of US presidential elections is relevant once again here. As shown above, they demonstrated that politicians do often get blamed for things that are entirely outside their control, including shark attacks and the weather. No sane political system would respond to this fact by attempting to institute a system for directing the behaviour of sharks or where the rain clouds go. Responding to unwarranted blame at the centre for poor local decisions is a less extreme version of the same flawed thought process. As control of all those local decisions is impossible, at best central politicians will be creating an illusion. What Achen and Bartels' work shows us is that even an effective illusion of that kind is unlikely to affect how voters react. Blame simply goes with the territory if bad things happen, regardless of what the politician has done, appears to have done or has not done. Whether or not that blame lands, and where, will be driven by the prior level of cultural connection and values alignment with the voters concerned.

Decisions that have to be made at the centre

The above discussion has focused on complex public services that have to be delivered directly to citizens, like those in Hilary Cottam's experiments. In these cases there seems to be a strong argument, rooted in our discussion of culture and values, for taking a more local approach. Moving both decision making and accountability for decision making closer to the front-line is more in tune with how policy actually works. There is, however, another category of policy to consider: policies where a single decision at the centre has a direct impact. In these cases, there is no delivery chain, and no street-level bureaucratic culture that affects what happens on the ground. The most obvious example of such a policy is a change in tax rates. When a Chancellor of the Exchequer announces in his (at the time of writing all UK Chancellors have been men) Budget speech that the tax on beer is going up, prices in the pubs change the next day. Spending formulas are another example. If a central government decides to change the amount of money per pupil that each school receives then delivery is extremely simple and the new amount simply passes directly into the budgets of schools across the country (exactly what they do as a result of the change is much more complicated and locally-determined).

There is a small set of decisions, like these ones, that can't be localised. Such decisions also offer a counter-example to the argument in Chapter 6 about focusing scrutiny of policy on what the policy means for culture and values. The policies in this category do convey messages about values (where taxes are raised or cut is a very direct signal about what activities a society sees as valuable) but they also have direct real impact on people in a way that the majority of policy announcements do not. Therefore, it is important in these cases to maintain scrutiny on the costs and benefits of policy choices as well as their place in a narrative about culture and values.

What, then, does a focus on culture and values have to tell us about how to see these national decisions about taxation and spending? While they are not subject to the same issues around how culture affects implementation, they are still often used and framed in terms of values and intended to have an effect on them. I clearly remember the arguments within the then coalition government in the United Kingdom about the desire on the Conservative side of the government to introduce a tax break for married couples. This was, fairly explicitly, responding to a constituency within the party who wanted to make a symbolic statement about the value of marriage. I doubt whether even its most ardent advocates believed that the £650 million involved, at roughly £230 per couple per year, would actually lead to a significant change in the marriage rate.[6] It was all about expressing a view on the desirable family form. In this case evaluation of the policy would ideally look at whether attitudes to marriage were changing at all as a result, as opposed to changes in actual behaviour.

Culture and values also play strongly into policy making around central tax and spending decisions by affecting how those decisions are perceived by the public. As with any policy, what people believe to be fair and reasonable in these allocations of resources is strongly driven by prior values alignment with the government making the decisions. A good demonstration of the power of values in how people think about spending comes from Kramer's (2016) study of attitudes to government and government spending in Wisconsin. She looked at the relationship between a set of cultural attitudes towards government (often highly negative – her study is called 'The Politics of Resentment') and government spending in different parts of the state. A reasonable hypothesis around the way this relationship would work would be that people in areas with lower government spending would recognise they were missing out in relative terms, realise that they were receiving worse services, and resent the government as a result. A government that wished to address the resentment would be able to do so by changing the funding formula to reallocate money.

What Kramer found, however, was the reverse. Certain people held resentful views about government for prior cultural reasons, with no connection to their actual experience of government services and resource allocation. If they did hold these views, they assumed that public funding was skewed away from them and towards other areas of the state, regardless of whether that was the case in reality. The policy-making challenge in Wisconsin was thus much more difficult. It was very unlikely that changing the funding system would address resentment. Instead it would be necessary to engage with the cultures driving resentment, which Kramer identifies as being tied in a significant degree to cultural differences between urban and rural Wisconsin and 'government' in a general sense being associated with the former. So although spending decisions do have direct impacts and delivery system culture is less of a consideration, understanding how those decisions interact with cultural assumptions is crucial if policy makers want to achieve their goals.

Localism with a structured process

This chapter has argued for greater local control of public policy decisions. Local control does not, however, have to equate to an absence of any process at all. It is possible to learn from what methods have worked in developing local solutions in other areas. While the solutions may be different and attuned to local needs, the tools and techniques required to develop them can have similarities. Rejecting the chance to learn from the ways in which others have developed successful local solutions would be taking localism to an absurd extreme.

Hilary Cottam's work, mentioned above, gives a good illustration of this point. Her experiments are driven by particular communities and individuals, with very high levels of autonomy for those working on the projects. However, she also sets out some broad principles about how to obtain the necessary local commitment and trust, learnt from experience of trying these ways of working in different contexts. She is clear that when the experiments are replicated in another neighbourhood they will not come out exactly the same, but what worked in one place can at least provide a starting point and some techniques for dealing with common problems.

Another example of applying a common process to different local situations is the '100 Day Challenge' used by Nesta, the UK innovation foundation, to address healthcare challenges.[7] This involves an intensive programme where people from different organisations work together to come up with new ways to tackle an intractable problem. The Challenge has been used in different places, and on issues as diverse as reducing delays in discharging patients from hospital and managing the risk that someone develops diabetes. However, underneath this diversity of issue and location sits a highly structured process. The team behind the Challenge have developed ways to organise experiments, use data and build relationships that are replicable and make it easier for different areas to implement a new more bottom-up approach successfully.

Conclusion

Greater localism does seem to be a good response to the importance of culture and values. The impact of front-line culture on delivery is best accommodated by enabling judgements to be made about how to deal with complexity. Centralised systems collide with cultural realities and need to be flexed in response. Tools and techniques for doing more localised policy development well are starting to emerge, and the objections to such approaches have been overplayed. Fears of a postcode lottery will not be addressed by central control: the reality is that even centralised systems cannot ensure homogeneity. It is true that central politicians may well be blamed for local failures. They will also be blamed for all sorts of other things that are not in their control and never can be, and will not be blamed for things that in fact are down to them.

Given that centralised accountability is broken in this way, it is not a reason to give up on the potential benefits of localism. We do need to recognise that there is a set of decisions that have, by their nature, to stay at the centre, but even in these cases understanding how they affect and interact with culture and values is essential for successful policy making.

10

Building organisations

Culture and values are not abstract concepts that float free on their own. They are held by people and situated within social structures. In the examples discussed throughout this book, from Geertz's Balinese cockfighters to the voters who backed Donald Trump despite not believing his claims about the Mexican border wall, we have talked about the culture and values held by various groups of people. One particular type of social structure that is relevant when considering policy implementation is whatever organisation or organisations are doing the implementing. Organisations carry culture. As discussed in Chapter 1, every organisation has a set of unwritten rules and practices and a set of values that it implicitly or explicitly promotes. Therefore one tool available to the policy maker who wishes to take culture seriously is to build organisations that embody the culture that they want to carry through.

Many organisations are explicit about the values and culture that they intend to stand for. This can be at the level of bland corporate value statements put up on walls and computer screen-savers. But it can also be taken much more seriously, for example in the most important choice any organisation makes, namely who gets to work there. There are many examples of organisations that explicitly recruit people on the basis of their personal alignment with the values that the organisation stands for. One of the most significant examples of this in the United Kingdom is the approach now taken by Health Education England, which has a whole programme on 'values based recruitment' for selecting the medical staff of the future.[1] My own current organisation, Big Society Capital, also has one part of its recruitment process that is specifically aimed at exploring a candidate's values.

Examples of building organisations

The financial services sector in the United Kingdom offers a good demonstration of the potential long-term impact of building organisations with a particular culture and values. From the late 18th century, 'building clubs' began to be established, which were jointly-owned co-operative groups that aimed to enable working or lower-middle class people to purchase or build their own homes (Scott and Newton, 2012). From the mid-19th century some of them developed into permanent mutually owned lending institutions, mainly with strong roots in a particular town or city. By the inter-war period these building societies were the 'dominant player in the house mortgage market' (Samy, 2012: 168) in the United Kingdom. The building societies had a particular culture, rooted in their history and mutual status, of low-risk practices and a focus on access to finance for the working classes (Samy, 2012). As Lewin (2002: 319) says, mutual organisations have 'an emphasis on reciprocity, commonality of interest, shared values and social purpose'.

During the 1980s and 1990s several of the building societies demutualised, transforming themselves into public limited companies and transferring shares to their former members. With this change in ownership came, in many cases, a change in culture and business practice. The most dramatic demonstration of this was the collapse of the former building society Northern Rock in 2007 after the first run on a UK retail bank since 1866 (Marshall et al, 2012). Subsequent investigations into what went wrong showed an organisation that had, in business culture, moved about as far as possible from the set of values described above as being associated with the mutual building societies. The Treasury Select Committee of the House of Commons (2008) found a culture of risk taking on very tight margins, over-confidence and reckless growth. Several other former building societies, such as the Bradford and Bingley, experienced similar failures during the 2008 financial crisis. In contrast those that had stayed mutual, including the largest building society (Nationwide), were largely insulated from the crisis. Their lending cultures and business priorities had not exposed them to the short-term funding sources that suddenly dried up when liquidity disappeared from global credit markets.

The building societies and their strong cultures were not created by conscious acts of policy making but by communities organising themselves to solve a problem (access to mortgage finance). Direct policy decisions can also be used to create organisations with a particular culture. A good set of examples comes from the experience in different countries with anti-corruption agencies. In these cases, reform-minded leaders have identified a problem with endemic corruption in parts of the public sector bureaucracy. They fear that the culture of corruption is such that any attempts to reduce it will be undermined by the existing institutions and the vested interests of the corrupt officials who control them. Therefore the policy makers look to establish separate external agencies to address corruption, building them with a clear focus on an anti-corruption culture and a set of values around probity.

It is reasonably commonplace to create such agencies. They are recommended by the United Nations Convention Against Corruption of 2003, and between 1995 and 2005 over 50 were established (Gemperle, 2018). In the anti-corruption field at least, creating new organisations as a way of tackling cultural barriers is a mainstream policy tool. This is not to say that it is an easy solution. Creating a new organisation with a distinctive culture in an environment that is likely to be hostile and operating by a different set of norms and values is always going to be challenging. Doig et al (2007) found in their review of new anti-corruption commissions that many struggled. While there were some notable success stories (Hong Kong is often cited), in other countries such as Zambia and Uganda the new institutions were less effective. This was often down to under-resourcing, tension between different aid donors who supported the anti-corruption drives, and challenges with staffing.

Different models of organisation building

The fact that many anti-corruption commissions struggle in their mission to build effective organisations with a new culture shows that we need to think through the different options for using institution building as a policy tool and when they are most likely to be effective. The examples above of the building societies and the anti-corruption commissions show that institution building as a policy can operate on different levels, depending on how directly the government wants to be involved.

The most direct option is to simply create a new government agency, as in most of the anti-corruption cases. Such an approach is relatively quick and gives the policy maker a high degree of control. However, it will only work when a centrally-controlled agency is a plausible route through to effective policy implementation. As we saw in Chapter 9, taking culture and values seriously implies that central control is only the answer in particular relatively rare situations. Whether this direct model will work also depends on what the desired culture in the delivery agency actually is. Top-down imposition may not work as a strategy for creating a free-thinking and entrepreneurial culture. Furthermore, an organisation that is created from the centre may well be equally easy to abolish from the centre if there is a change of political control. To secure a legacy that lasts beyond a single administration, a more dispersed approach may be necessary.

Therefore policy makers will sometimes work at another level: creating an overall system where public service delivery organisations with a new culture can emerge and thrive. This may involve altering regulations and the funding regime, and providing the basic guidance and legal forms for establishing different organisational types. The organisations themselves are not directly created by the central government.

An example of this approach is the academy schools programme in England. In 2000 the then Secretary of State for Education, David Blunkett, announced the programme as a way of tackling persistently under-performing schools, primarily in inner-city areas. (The programme was initially known as 'City

Academies'.) The policy has been taken on and expanded by successive governments and by summer 2019 there were roughly 8,000 academies in England.[2] Academies are independent of local government control, and while they receive funding directly from central government they have considerable freedom. They are, for example, able to diverge from the national curriculum and hire staff on terms and conditions that fall outside national arrangements negotiated with the teaching unions. One of the major goals of the policy, and these additional freedoms, was to create schools with a different culture of leadership, empowered to attempt different strategies to deliver improved outcomes for pupils. As the Department for Education put it in 2005, the aim was for these new schools to be 'leaders in innovation' (DfES, 2005).

There is considerable debate about whether the freedoms given to academics have delivered improved educational outcomes or not, and whether the programme has represented value for money. I am not going to attempt to resolve these arguments here.[3] What is more important from the perspective of this discussion is whether there has been an impact on culture. Have policy makers succeeded in creating a new class of public service delivery organisations with a different culture, whether or not that culture has had the benefits that they claimed it would?

As discussed in Chapter 7, although culture change is often an explicit policy objective it is frequently not included in the factors to be evaluated when considering whether the policy is a success. In the case of the academies programme, the weight of evaluation has been around the impact on pupil performance, with less attention paid to whether a new type of school culture has been developed. One attempt to look at the impact on culture and ethos was made after the early phase of the academy programme (Woods et al, 2007). This study looked at one specific aspect of culture, namely what the authors called 'entrepreneurialism', described as the quality of an organisational culture that attempts to achieve its ends by innovation and using resources in new ways. It concluded that there was a demonstrable difference in the new academies towards a greater culture of entrepreneurialism. A more recent study (Chapman, 2013) considered the impact of the academy programme on leadership cultures in schools, and concluded that in some cases there had been a significant impact but this was patchy and depended on the local context. So there is some evidence of an impact on culture but it is not clear-cut despite the sustained roll-out of academies. This model, of creating a system context that enables organisations with the desired culture to thrive, is an interesting policy tool but requires a long implementation period and will tend to be hard to see through.

There is a third model of organisation building that is even less direct. In the academies example, although the new schools are more autonomous they still operate within a framework that is controlled by the government and deliver a service that is entirely funded from the public purse. The third model is where government policy aims to facilitate the creation of completely independent entities, operating in markets or systems that are not entirely government controlled. It is still possible for government to have a view about the culture of independent organisations and to promote the success of those that have the delivery culture most in line with policy objectives.

At the time of writing I have been working for Big Society Capital, an independent institution with the goal of connecting investment capital to organisations with a social purpose. These organisations are mainly charities and social enterprises, set up to tackle social challenges and with a strong set of values behind what they do. As they grow, these organisations will only succeed if they grow a caring and ethical culture along the way (Andre and Pache, 2016). We at Big Society Capital are working with partners to try to bring those caring cultures into economic sectors where we feel they are sorely needed. For example we worked with the Joseph Rowntree Foundation to create Fair by Design, a programme to invest in socially-motivated businesses that are entering markets where people in poverty tend to pay unfair additional costs. Financial services such as credit, insurance and rent-to-own appliances are good examples.

The UK government has recognised that there are public benefits to initiatives like these that aim to bring organisations with different values and cultures into the business of delivering public services and wider public benefit. The charity and social enterprise sector is, by definition, independent. Policy makers cannot decide where social enterprise will play a role. What they can do, however, is create an environment where those socially-minded organisations can flourish. For example, in 2014 the UK Government created the Social Investment Tax Relief[4] which provides an incentive for people to invest in social enterprises by allowing people to claim a 30 per cent income tax relief in certain circumstances, and was later ranked as the 4th best tax relief in Europe by an independent study (PriceWaterhouseCoopers, 2017).

Another example is the Public Services (Social Value) Act of 2012,[5] which required public agencies to consider environmental and social wellbeing when they are letting contracts. Some local authorities have used the mechanism that this legislation provides to encourage a greater presence of social enterprises in their supply chains, believing that the different delivery culture they will experience as a result will benefit the community. For example, Salford in Greater Manchester has gone beyond the strict requirements of the Act to include social enterprises within its work as far as possible, leading to it being designated a 'social enterprise city' by the social enterprise sector's membership body.[6]

When will organisation building work?

The three models of organisation building in support of policy objectives fit different circumstances, depending on the level of government control that is both desirable and feasible. We also need to ask when organisation building is appropriate at all. Creating a new organisation can be an effective way to turn cultural change into reality. It is also very risky, as the mixed experience of the anti-corruption commissions in different countries shows. There are three main points to bear in mind when considering whether organisation building is likely to be an effective strategy.

The first is whether organisational level decision making is a critical variable in the area of policy under consideration. We noted above that culture and values always sit within a social context. However, that context does not always need to be an organisation. In the examples considered so far in this chapter, the organisational level is indeed critical: how a school approaches its curriculum; what approach to risk a bank or building society has; how a local council procures services. Some policy areas do not look like this, and instead individual citizen-level decision making is key. Public health issues like diet, exercise or substance misuse are good examples. Cultural change is still vital for making progress on those issues, as people will not improve their diets or go to the gym as a result of legislation. It is just that the cultural norms that are most powerful in determining these types of individual behaviour are carried by families and peer groups rather than government institutions. A policy maker might be able to change the way public health interventions are delivered by creating a new local health organisation with a different ethos, but that is one step removed from the community-level culture change that is the essential agreement in tackling this kind of issue.

The second point to bear in mind is whether an institution needs to be directly democratically accountable. Different societies make different choices about the extent to which the leaders of certain types of organisations need to be elected. At one end of the spectrum are absolutist regimes that elect no-one at all, while at the other end parts of the United States elect officials to what in Europe would be seen as specialised bureaucratic posts. For example, Texas elects members of a Railroads Commission, California an Insurance Commissioner and Arizona elects a State Mines Inspector. Whatever position a given country has come to about which areas of policy need to be subject to direct election, there will be implications for the use of organisation building as a policy tool. This is because it is hard to build a new organisational culture when that is subject to immediate change depending on the decisions taken at the ballot box. Organisations will adapt to the prevailing political leadership and the view of the majority (or the largest minority, depending on the electoral system) rather than embedding a particular set of values over time.

The possible exception to this argument is if the intention of the policy maker was to instil in the new organisation a culture of responsiveness to elections and changing political leadership. It may be the case that there was previously a culture of stasis over time or elite capture, and direct accountability is a potential way to create a new more responsive culture. One recent example of this thinking in the United Kingdom was the creation of elected Police and Crime Commissioners to replace the old appointed Police Authorities. Low turnout for the elections (just 15.1 per cent in the first elections in 2012; Hill, 2014) raises serious questions over the success of this approach in that instance.

The third point for the policy maker to consider is what level of competition a new organisation faces. No new entity starts in a vacuum. Existing players will see a potential challenge and mobilise accordingly. In the case of the anti-corruption commissions, one of the problems in some of the cases where the new body was less successful was the way in which the existing bureaucracy managed to neutralise its effectiveness (Doig et al, 2007). Competition should not put the policy maker off entirely, however. The culture and values of a new organisation may give it a competitive advantage. As shown above, the building society movement managed to carve out a major role in the United Kingdom's financial services industry, through a combination of identifying a market niche that others did not understand and having an ethos that was inherently attractive. A more recent example of success in a highly competitive market comes from the Fair Trade movement. Fair Trade brought a new value-set to coffee and cocoa industries, giving a higher priority to the income and welfare of producers in developing countries. This set of values gave Fair Trade organisations a new and compelling customer proposition, and Fair Trade had grown to sales of US$9.2 billion by 2017.[7]

Conclusion

Organisation building will not work in all circumstances. Policy makers need to consider whether organisational culture is a critical part of achieving their goal, if the vagaries of elections are likely to knock the long and painful work of organisation building off track and whether the competitive landscape will permit a new body to flourish. They also need to consider whether to create new organisations directly, or to attempt to create a climate for organisations with certain cultures to thrive. With those caveats in place, creating a new organisation remains an important option for creating cultural change. An organisation that lives and espouses a powerful culture and set of values has great potential to make a difference.

11

Being smart about evidence

Discussions about policy often move quickly into discussions about evidence. In the mid-1990s, when I was starting out in my policy career, the concept of 'evidence-based policy-making' was very much in vogue. The UK Government published the White Paper *Modernising Government* (Cabinet Office, 1999). It called for policies 'shaped by the evidence' and measured by 'results rather than activity' (1999: 15). In a section entitled 'What Must Change' the White Paper highlighted 'better use of evidence and research' as one of the top priorities (1999: 16). The Performance and Innovation Unit (forerunner of the Prime Minister's Strategy Unit where I later worked) was established in 1998 in part to bring a renewed focus on evidence and analysis to the centre of government. From 2013 onwards the then government developed a network of specialist What Works Centres, responsible for driving evidence and understanding in particular fields. By 2018 there were ten, covering issues from ageing to education to social care (Cabinet Office, 2018). Other countries have developed similar networks (such as the What Works Cities group in the United States).

The chapter addresses the question of how a focus on culture and values sits alongside the value of evidence in policy making. Is it possible to combine rigour around data and evidence with a proper reflection of the importance of softer elements like culture? How does evidence operate in the values-driven political and policy environment set out in Parts One and Two of this book, and what does that mean for how the policy maker needs to think about evidence?

How does evidence work in the policy process?

The starting point for this discussion has to be an understanding of what role evidence plays in the policy process. I remember on the first day of my Public Policy Master's course being shown a diagram of the 'policy cycle'. This is the model that will be familiar to many students and practitioners of policy: a circle that starts with agenda setting, moving to policy formulation, adoption through the political process, implementation, evaluation and back to agenda setting again.[1] In this model, evidence plays a clear role. The policy maker uses evidence to formulate their policy, gathers new evidence through the evaluation stage and then uses that new material to formulate the next policy iteration.

My lecturer that day, Wayne Parsons, was actually a sceptic about the value of the policy cycle model. As he explained to us during the rest of the course, and as he has also set out in his research, it is a serious over-simplification of how policy is developed and the role that evidence plays. Parsons (2002) assesses what actually happened as a result of the *Modernising Government* White Paper and the attempt in the United Kingdom to increase the use of evidence-based policy. He argues that the evidence-based policy movement was premised on the view that there was a clear body of knowledge that would enable government to steer policy in a strategic way. The movement also assumed that this knowledge could be considered in a managerial and non-political way. Parsons concludes that both practical experience, and theory from public policy scholars such as Lasswell, demonstrates that the idea of stable non-contested evidence is a mirage. Complex social situations that governments need to wrestle with are constantly changing and the legitimacy of different forms of evidence is a political matter rather than one for neutral academic assessment.

Cairney (2016, 2017) makes a similar argument. His book is called *The Politics of Evidence-Based Policy-Making*, emphasising the point that evidence is part of a political and rather messy process rather than something separate with a superior claim on the policy makers' attention. Cairney makes two critical points about how evidence is used in a policy system. The first is that what counts as 'evidence' in a policy context is often unclear. 'Evidence-based policy' as a concept has a clear relationship to the longer standing concept of 'evidence-based medicine'. The gold standard of evidence accepted by the medical profession is randomised controlled trials, peer-reviewed, published in leading journals and (ideally) replicated. For most policy questions there is not, and is never likely to be, evidence of this standard (Cairney, 2017). While randomised controlled trials have been increasing as a policy-making tool, there remain only a minority of situations where they are possible or useful (Page, 2016). Therefore policy makers are required to use a much greater variety of evidence from different sources and with different levels of academic rigour. What counts as worthwhile evidence in a given policy context is subjective. It depends on both the requirements of a particular situation (such as the timeframes available to gather information) and also the norms and expectations of the policy-making institution involved. The role that norms play in determining what counts as useful evidence in a particular context brings culture in to determining how evidence affects policy.

Cairney's (2017) second point is around how decision makers who are faced with complex situations use evidence. He draws on analyses of different policy processes by other scholars to identify ways in which evidence is used in policy making that bear little relationship to the neat flow implied by the policy cycle. Some of these ways are very relevant to our focus on culture and values. Cairney identifies that political leaders use facts and evidence not as a neutral input to deliberation but to illustrate and strengthen stories they have already decided to use in order to make emotional values-based appeals to particular groups in society. Evidence being used as an input to and reinforcement for pre-existing planned messages is a phenomenon very familiar from my time as a senior civil servant. I became used to speeches emerging from ministerial speech writers with square brackets at a particular point in the text and a request along the lines of 'insert supportive fact here'. Here evidence was being used as a tool to support a strategy or story, not to determine it in advance.

Cairney also notes that policy makers interpret facts and evidence in the light of their existing beliefs. As discussed in Chapter 7, voters suffer from confirmation bias whereby facts that accord with their pre-existing mental frameworks will be given more psychological weight than those which do not. The phenomenon of confirmation bias does not just apply to voters but to policy makers too. Evidence is filtered in accordance with how it aligns with their pre-conceived views of the world. These views may be ideological and tied to a particular political perspective, but could also be broader cultural assumptions about, for example, what is socially acceptable. The idea of an impartial policy-making system that weighs evidence in a neutral manner, devoid of any such frameworks, is unrealistic given what we know about how human psychology actually operates.

The third point that Cairney raises is that policy makers are always constrained by what is feasible. At any time they face a particular set of funding constraints, power structures, public opinion and political authority. Therefore they require a policy that can fit through the 'policy window' (Kingdon, 1984) that is open at the relevant moment, determined by these and other factors. Evidence is useful in as much as it helps to design something with that fit. The best evidence in the world is of little value if it is not timely to when the 'window' opens, or it points in a direction that, for example, isn't deliverable within a pre-agreed and fixed budget. I can illustrate this point with an example from my experience at Big Society Capital, the social investment organisation. The funds we work with often invest in charities and social enterprises that have developed interventions with great potential for preventing social problems from emerging or getting worse. Examples include intensive work with families that prevents vulnerable children from requiring residential care, and 'social prescribing' where doctors refer people to non-medical services run by community groups that help them manage long-term conditions in a way that reduces hospital admissions. Many of these interventions have a strong evidence base and a track record that they can make a difference to the people concerned, as well as saving money for the public sector. Those savings, however, generally accrue over several years as downstream costs (for example, in hospitals) are avoided. Such evidence of savings is often of little use to local service commissioners who have immediate cash pressures in their budgets: it is very hard for them to invest additional resource now which they don't have, even if it saves money later. The window that they have is for policies that reduce costs immediately, and evidence pointing to such savings is what would have an impact.

The above discussion shows that culture and values are an important consideration in understanding how evidence interacts with policy making in practice. Which evidence is influential and how depends on context. Evidence does not land from the academy onto a blank canvas, but into an environment with prior beliefs and values, and a prior set of objectives and possibilities. Culture and values are not the only driver of that context, of course. Formal institutional factors (such as resources and procedures) matter as well as informal culture. The relative political power of different actors is also significant, in particular for determining what is feasible in terms of a policy window as in the example above. All these factors combine to create the environment in which evidence plays a role.

What evidence do policy makers need?

The richer understanding of how evidence interacts with other factors in the policy process that Cairney and Parsons set out has implications for what approaches to generating evidence are most useful. It is possible to draw out four conclusions that will help guide those producing evidence, whether academics, think-tanks or government researchers, to the approaches that will lead to the greatest level of use by policy makers and therefore the greatest impact.

The first conclusion relates to Cairney's point about what counts as sufficient evidence. As noted above, the level of standardised rigour applied to medical treatments does not easily translate into most areas of political decision making. The level of evidence needed depends on the context and the level of trust the policy maker is asked to place in it. Nesta attempted to make these judgements about what counts as 'good' evidence clearer and more systematic in their report *Standards of Evidence* (Puttick and Ludlow, 2013). The standards set out a way that evidence can range from just a set of logical and coherent assumptions about what a policy intervention is achieving, through different levels of data that demonstrate an assumption may be valid through to tested methods for replicating the original effect. The report is clear that there is not a single right answer about how much evidence is needed. The lowest level is entirely appropriate in some situations, for example 'early stage interventions, that may still be at the idea stage' (Puttick and Ludlow, 2013: 2). The Nesta standards are just one example, but they effectively illustrate the choices that are available in deciding what evidence to produce and why, focusing on the needs and the context of the person expected to act upon it. The producer of evidence needs to think through the standard that their potential customers might need.

The second conclusion is the importance of considering the role of evidence within a narrative. As discussed above, evidence is often used to strengthen an emotional appeal that resonates with the underlying values of the audience. The 'insert fact here' experience that I mentioned is often exasperating for government officials who are trying to work with a sophisticated understanding of complex evidence. Ultimately, however, given what we have seen in previous chapters about the political power of cultural narratives, evidence will need to be presented in a way that it can play a useful part in an environment where those narratives are dominant. It is possible to use evidence in a way that is both honest and has emotional resonance in the relevant cultural context. Al Gore's film *An Inconvenient Truth* is a good example, combining a nuanced and credible account of climate science with a powerful values-based appeal. Those who produce the evidence need to be prepared to engage in a process of making it usable for storytelling, bridging the gap between research that seeks objectivity and the subjective, symbolic and often simplistic world of communications.

The third conclusion is linked to the second in that it addresses how evidence can be communicated. We saw above how policy makers use shortcuts to navigate complex information, and will prioritise pieces of evidence that fit neatly with either specific prior beliefs or their overall world-view. Simplicity is again one way to respond to this: it will be easier for busy policy makers to assimilate evidence if it is possible to grasp the key points in a straightforward way. In the United Kingdom, the funding councils that support academic research have started to recognise the importance of being able to communicate research to a lay audience. Statements on the 'Pathway to Impact' of each research proposal are now mandatory.[2] Returning to culture, the expectations in the academic community about how research should be presented and discussed are rather different from many policy-making contexts. The more these two worlds can understand one another's values and behaviours, the more likely that evidence will have traction given the prevailing policy mindsets.

The fourth conclusion relates to the 'policy windows' outlined above. At any given time the ways in which institutions, power and resources align mean that some policy developments are possible and some are not. In practice, this process tends to produce what Baumgartner and Jones (1993) famously called 'punctuated equilibrium': a situation where most policy fields see long periods where there is little change punctuated by large and sometimes random-seeming shifts.

We can think about the implications for evidence of both the equilibrium and the moments of punctuation. In the periods of relative equilibrium (which is most policy areas most of the time) overall policy is not changing. What is always changing, however, are the incremental details of practical action as individuals and organisations adapt what they do in the light of experience. The important type of evidence, therefore, is small-scale, practical and shows its value quickly. As a recent report on health policy innovation in the United Kingdom put it, 'Above all, we have found that improving health and financial outcomes rests far more on whether a practice and culture of continuous improvement is established, rather than the strength of the evidence informing the original investment case' (Social Finance, 2019: 15). That practice and culture of continuous improvement requires evidence, but simple, rapid and practical evidence rather than the comprehensive analysis that would have sat behind the investment business case. Cairney and Oliver (2017) call this kind of evidence-informed responsive practice 'learning as you go'. When designing research, it would be worth considering whether the outputs are likely to be helpful for practitioners trying to find ways to make incremental improvements within a broadly static policy equilibrium, as this is the most common situation.

The punctuation moments, when political or other events create a moment of major policy instability, are by their nature unpredictable and hard to plan for. It is unlikely that the window of change will happen to open just at the time a major research project has been completed to create soundly evidence-based policies of just the type that suits what everyone is looking for. Instead, those who are creating the evidence base for new policies need to accept that the moments of change can arrive seemingly at random. What matters is to have evidence ready to support policy change in an opportunistic way when the time is right. As Chapter 6 explained, the detail of a policy is often less important than its symbolic value. Therefore, when a window of opportunity is created by some external event, the policy change that is enacted as a result need not be directly tied to that event. Instead, it needs to speak to the set of values and concerns that the event evokes among the electorate or interested pressure groups. Therefore it is worth devising evidence for policies that may seem unlikely to ever speak directly to an imperative for action.

I heard a good example of this strategy recently at a discussion between civil society organisations about influencing policy.[3] One group there had spent years developing a fairly technical policy that would have an impact on a certain business sector. Something happened that made targeting that sector politically desirable. While their policy had nothing at all to do with the event itself, and would not prevent it from happening again, the fact that they had a well-evidenced and credible policy aimed at what was politically-speaking the right target meant that it suddenly gained major support. It spoke to the values that were being prioritised at that moment. Evidence is, therefore, part of being prepared to seize unpredictable opportunity and should be developed with that use in mind.

Is evidence itself values-based?

The previous sections considered how best to think about the place of evidence in policy making in the light of the previous findings on how culture and values affect that process. This section considers a different angle: the extent to which appealing to evidence is in itself a values-laden concept.

The role of evidence and expertise in policy making and politics came into sharp focus during the 2016 referendum on the United Kingdom's membership of the European Union. Michael Gove, then a leading figure in the Leave campaign, responded to reports that leaving the Union would reduce economic growth by saying 'I think the people in this country have had enough of experts'.[4] Culture and values help us to understand why he might make this claim and why many people might agree with him. Evidence is often provided and discussed by a particular professional class (in this case academic economists). If that class look and sound culturally alien to many voters, then their message is less likely to be taken seriously. Calling for greater use of evidence in a policy debate is not a value-neutral statement. It is also a way of signalling where someone stands in relation to a particular set of values, in particular the values associated with whichever professional class determines what counts as 'evidence' in that context. In part it is the claims of professional experts to embody some kind of objective neutrality that alienates people who do not agree with them and who feel they represent a different culture. Commitment to culture is always likely to be stronger than commitment to follow a set of evidence, in the same way that Chapter 6 demonstrated that it can also override commitment to norms of democratic behaviour. Therefore people will often see a plea to 'look at the evidence' as a plea to change something that feels fundamental to them to suit the wishes of a culturally-alien 'expert'.

I experienced this phenomenon of an appeal to evidence being interpreted as giving preference to a set of professional values in my time in the Ministry of Justice. As civil servants we were all aware of the extensive evidence base around prison sentences. In particular many pieces of internal and external research showed that short prison sentences were associated with higher levels of reoffending than community punishments for the same offence. We also saw that the data demonstrated that longer prison sentences had no impact on public confidence in the criminal justice system. The evidence here was of a high standard, replicated repeatedly in several studies over different time periods. However, several Members of Parliament and much of the media took a different view. Any reference by a government spokesperson or external expert to this body of work was taken as demonstrating not that policy should change, but that they were defying 'common sense' and were clearly 'out of touch' with how the mass of the public understood crime and punishment. Unsurprisingly, little of this evidence found its way into policy.

Examples like this indicate that calling for 'evidence-based policy' may not be a politically successful formula. It is interesting that the Blair government was so overt about this as a priority, probably because moving beyond ideology was a central plank of the Blair narrative. Somewhat ironically, therefore, evidence-based policy making was here playing a symbolic role in constructing a narrative rather than necessarily changing how government worked in reality. For a contrasting example, where an appeal to evidence sent a message that contributed to political failure, we can look at the 2019 presidential election in Sri Lanka. Sajith Premasanda called during the campaign for policy making to be a 'rational process'[5] and to 'introduce guided and structured decision-making processes where relevant statistics and substances are used'.[6] In the end this technocratic message about evidence appears to have been out of tune with many of the voters and came second to Gotobaya Rajapaska's campaign based on emotive appeals to security and Sinhalese ethnic identity.

The fact that evidence is not stronger than culture, and how it is received depends on the congruence of culture and values between those presenting and receiving it, does not undermine the use of evidence in policy making entirely. Instead, it reinforces some of the messages from the previous section. Thinking about the context evidence will land in, the world-views and preconceptions of the listeners, and what is possible for them given their value-sets will all help increase the chance of that congruence. The messenger and the cultural cues they convey is important as well as the message for understanding the likely impact on politics and policy.

Evidence from other countries

This final section looks at a specific question on the use of evidence in policy making: learning from evidence created by experience with related policy in other countries. Chapter 2 set out how culture and values affect policy outcomes, and discussed research from the World Bank (2008b) and the Institute of Development Studies (2010) that demonstrated that informal cultural differences tend to undermine efforts to use policy solutions from one country in another. The example of the Indonesian cities in that chapter showed that even within a country replicating policy often doesn't lead to the same results.

Despite this experience, taking evidence from overseas remains a popular approach in policy making. In the Prime Minister's Strategy Unit we used to have a standing joke that whenever we were asked to investigate a new policy question we should just look up what was happening in Denmark, as there was bound to be a policy there that at least appeared to be an improvement on the current situation in the United Kingdom. British policy makers are also often keen to learn from the United States. One policy that many politicians were keen to import across the Atlantic was the Family Nurse Partnership. Developed by David Olds at the University of Colorado, this programme provided intensive support at home to low-income mothers (Olds, 2006). The results were impressive, showing improvements in parental care practice and also benefits for the future life course of the mother as measured by factors such as employment and need for welfare provision. The Department of Health launched a small pilot in England, followed by a wider roll-out to 9,000 expectant mothers (Barnes, 2010) and then wider development.

Results in the English model of Family Nurse Partnerships did not immediately live up to the expectations generated by success in the United States. Robling et al (2016: 146) concluded that

'Adding FNP [Family Nurse Partnership] to the usually provided health and social care provided no additional short-term benefit to our primary outcomes. Programme continuation is not justified on the basis of available evidence'. In another study, the authors concluded that the English iteration of the programme was not a cost-effective intervention when considering its impact alongside that of services that already existed (Corbacho et al, 2017). Something had been lost in translation in moving the policy across the Atlantic and re-creating it in the very different institutional and cultural context of the United Kingdom.

So should policy makers simply try to resist the temptation to copy policy ideas from elsewhere, and look for evidence closer to home and more relevant to their own cultural context? Trying to replicate specific policies does look like a fool's errand, based on experience to date. Where there is some potential value is to look at a higher level question. Instead of asking 'can we implement the policy that was successful in country X?' we can ask 'what is it about the system in country X that enabled them to create and implement such a successful policy?' (Andrews, 2013). Asking the question this way points us towards the culture that enabled the successful policy to emerge, alongside other important factors. It is harder for a policy maker to try to replicate the system properties and culture that led to successful policy creation than to simply implement a version of the policy in their own jurisdiction. It is, however, much more likely to succeed.

Conclusion

Evidence can be combined with a good understanding of culture and values. A successful combination requires a nuanced view of evidence, understanding how it is used in the policy-making process and where it interfaces with narrative, symbols, culture and the unpredictable vagaries of political opportunity. People creating evidence for policy need to reflect on how it will be understood and communicated. They also need to put more effort into practical rapidly available evidence to incrementally improve practice, as that is the reality of policy change in most areas most of the time. The cultural baggage that comes with an appeal to evidence is also real and colours how it will be received.

Conclusion

This book has presented a case, based on my experience and research by others, that culture and values need to be at the heart of thinking about policy making. I am not claiming that this is the only lens through which policy making can be viewed, or that taking such a view solves all the challenges a policy maker can face. Instead, I hope you agree that thinking about policy without reflecting on these factors risks missing out important elements, and putting culture and values closer to the centre of our world-view will help explain why efforts to change policy turn out the way they do.

As I said in the Introduction, the recommendations for what policy makers should do differently are necessarily tentative, as they draw heavily on my own experience, which is largely in the context of central government, the wider public sector and civil society organisations in the United Kingdom. Other parts of the policy-making system and other countries will create different challenges in which culture and values play out in different ways. Naturally, in keeping with the overall approach of this book, I would advise the reader to take my suggestions as a starting point for developing policy-making practice consistent with their own values and the culture in which they are operating.

My first and most important conclusion is about clarity and honesty. Recognising when a debate or a decision rests on culture and values and being transparent about that is a prerequisite for a healthy political culture. I believe that many debates that are currently conducted in the language of feasibility and cost are actually about fairness, justice and prioritisation of interests. Policies are often evaluated against technocratic criteria while they are really aimed at sending a message or constructing a narrative. We have set up a framework of accountability that requests and then provides information that is irrelevant to the values-based decisions that voters and policy makers actually take. So I think that to put culture and values at the heart of policy making we first need to recognise that they are there already and be up-front and honest about the role they play. Without this, it will be hard to make progress on the other ideas.

The other conclusions are more about how to improve policy-making practice if we have taken this first step. One is about the kind of information that is going to be most useful for driving policy improvement. I would like to see a shift of resources from large-scale evaluation of policy programmes to the provision of granular front-line data in as near to real-time as possible and in a way that is as useful as possible to practitioners. The rationale for this shift is two-fold. First, we have seen that a culture of continuous improvement at the front-line is probably the single most important factor in long-term policy success. Second, the central policy-making apparatus is not capable of using detailed evaluations to drive policy change and not incentivised to do so, given what we know about what drives political choice.

A closely linked conclusion is that, with a few exceptions, there is a strong case for greater devolution of control of public policy. The point above on practical improvement at the front-line stands as an argument in favour of a more local approach. As Chapter 9 set out in detail, once we put culture and values at the centre of our thinking about public policy, the major objections to a more local approach (the fear of a 'postcode lottery' and the fear that central government politicians will be held to account for local failure) fall away.

I also identified some policy tools that should be given greater prominence. Governments can and do affect culture and values in the society they serve, whether they like it or not and whether they intend to do so or it happens as a by-product. Therefore I think the responsible course of action is to develop expertise in the ways in which this happens, a professional culture of learning and improvement and the relevant tools. In my experience the core disciplines used to train policy makers and implementers at the moment are economics, law, project management and some statistics. None of these are the most helpful background for thinking systematically and effectively about culture and values. I think the public administrations of the future need to enhance their capability in anthropology, psychology, communications (beyond media handling into building long-term narratives and symbols) and, given we are talking about values, potentially even philosophy.

The other tool I emphasised was about building organisations. The power of an organisation to embody and perpetuate a culture and a set of values is a great asset to be used. Governments create organisations all the time, but often not with an eye to the culture they need to promote. The organisation-building strategy is also not just about creating new government bodies, but creating a wider environment where organisations of particular types, with particular cultures, can flourish or take on new roles.

My recommendations for doing policy differently of course face all the challenges that this book has identified as facing any policy recommendations. Saying that policy makers should take culture and values seriously is itself not a value-neutral statement. It presumes that such an approach is within acceptable bounds, and that the outcomes I describe are valuable. An appeal to culture and values risks the same pitfall that I identified as being attached to an appeal to evidence: it may simply come across as an appeal to prioritise the view of people like me, from a culture of being interested in culture. I accept this challenge, and recognise that therefore not everyone will be convinced. But I hope that the stories and evidence in this book inspire some people working in policy, in whatever capacity, to try to do things differently.

Notes

Chapter 1

[1] There is a school of thought that a distinction between policy makers and other actors in society is a false one, and implies a rarefied elite who make policy and then hand it down to other social actors. I accept there is considerable truth in this argument, and for the purpose of the distinction drawn in this chapter I am not assuming that the role of 'policy maker' is limited to the formal institutions of government. Who is involved in policy making depends on context.

[2] For example, McAndrew et al (2019) found that workers in the cultural industries are the most left-wing, liberal and pro-welfare of any occupations and industries, and were unusually heavily engaged in political activity.

Chapter 2

[1] I discovered that the paper is not actually made from real goat but is instead a modern version named after the old practice of writing on parchment made from animal skin.

[2] There is considerable and unresolved debate about whether Drucker did actually coin this famous phrase. There are alternative claims about its origin. For a sense of this debate see https://quoteinvestigator.com/2017/05/23/culture-eats/

Chapter 3

[1] For an example of this kind of external pressure see www.theguardian.com/law/2017/mar/15/governments-1bn-plan-for-online-courts-challenges-open-justice

[2] Literally so, in my experience. The first lecture in my first week of studying philosophy as an undergraduate at Oxford was about the differences between these two conceptions of fairness and justice.

Chapter 4

[1] https://api.parliament.uk/historic-hansard/commons/1868/jul/13/observations

[2] For examples of these sorts of debates about league tables from different ideological standpoints see www.theguardian.com/commentisfree/2019/jan/26/school-league-tables-research-grammar and www.telegraph.co.uk/

education/secondaryeducation/9038770/School-league-tables-causing-drop-in-standards.html
3 This has been the case since 1981 in England, but not until the mid-1990s in other major football playing countries including Italy, Germany, France and Spain: another example of how different countries take different positions. Information on football league scoring systems taken from Wikipedia pages for each league, July 2018.
4 'Whiff of Sensation Hits New York', *Daily Telegraph*, 2 October 1999.
5 https://rediscovering-black-history.blogs.archives.gov/2016/10/25/voting-rights-in-the-early-1960s-registering-who-they-wanted-to/
6 Author's own analysis of election slogans; source material from https://en.wikipedia.org/wiki/List_of_U.K._political_slogans and https://en.wikipedia.org/wiki/List_of_U.S._presidential_campaign_slogans

Chapter 5
1 Including, for example, six European Film Awards including Best Film. All information from imdb.com.

Chapter 6
1 www.newstatesman.com/politics/june2017/2017/05/who-leaked-labours-manifesto
2 https://yougov.co.uk/topics/politics/articles-reports/2015/09/23/cabinet-recognition
3 Populus interviews a nationally representative sample of at least 2,000 British adults aged 18 and over each week, and asks what news story they had noticed the most. The question is open-ended and participants can name any story. www.populus.co.uk/insights/2018/12/brexit-tops-the-news-agenda-but-it-doesnt-mean-people-are-interested/
4 There is debate about whether he actually ever said this, or if so what exact words he used. See Knowles (2006: vi, 33).
5 Capara et al (2006) do also note that there are several mechanisms that link values and personality traits, and that other studies have demonstrated moderate levels of empirical correlation between them.
6 The term was first used by Goodwin and Ford in their 2014 book *Revolt on the Right*. However, Ford and Goodwin are very clear that they are not referring only to economic exclusion, but also to cultural exclusion, a point often lost in subsequent uses of the term by others.
7 https://uk.reuters.com/article/uk-britain-eu-coast-insight/in-brexit-on-sea-the-left-behind-still-want-out-idUKKCN1RG0GL
8 www.theguardian.com/commentisfree/2019/may/23/austerity-brexit-suffering-eu-anger
9 www.newstatesman.com/politics/uk/2019/03/there-ll-be-uprising-hartlepool-life-brexit-town-no-deal-sight
10 The gap was slightly different at different income levels, hence the 20–25 point range rather than a single number.

11 Data taken from https://ballotpedia.org/Pivot_Counties:_The_counties_ that_voted_Obama-Obama-Trump_from_2008-2016. Also see www. businessinsider.com/counties-flipped-from-obama-to-trump-struggling-economically-study-2019-6?r=US&IR=T

12 Data from www.cnbc.com/heres-a-map-of-the-us-counties-that-flipped-to-trump-from-democrats/

13 Text taken from official White House website: www.whitehouse.gov/ briefings-statements/the-inaugural-address/

Chapter 7

1 www.itv.com/news/2019-05-16/probation-service-to-supervise-all-offenders-after-flawed-privatisation/

2 www.bsa.natcen.ac.uk/downloads/questionnaires.aspx

3 The Institute for Government coined the term 'take out the trash day' for this opportunity for governments to bury a large number of potentially difficult announcements.

4 www.england.nhs.uk/fft/

5 The World Bank's 'Govtech' programme includes real-time communication between citizen and government to foster accountability as one of its key objectives: www.worldbank.org/en/topic/governance/brief/govtech-putting-people-first

Chapter 8

1 For example, George Osborne's words discussed in a piece by the think-tank Policy Exchange: https://policyexchange.org.uk/fixing-the-roof-while-the-sun-is-shining-osbornes-new-spending-rule/

2 https://fsi.stanford.edu/publicproblemsolving/docs/statement-education-public-problem-solving

Chapter 9

1 https://hansard.parliament.uk/Commons/2003-11-12/debates/7d0810da-d5af-486a-aeb7-423d341f8f9b/ChildSupportAgency – Intervention by Michael Moore.

2 For example, as measured by the level of taxation raised by sub-national levels of government: see King (2006).

3 A striking illustration of this came in some analysis I did of turnout in local government elections compared to in ballots about whether or not to transfer council housing to housing associations. The transfer ballots created huge engagement, with turnouts of well over 80 per cent being commonplace. In the same areas local council elections would often see under half of that. When a specific question with a direct impact on an important issue (housing) was in play, participation dramatically increased.

4 The definition of 'postcode lottery' in the *Cambridge English Dictionary* notes that it is a UK phrase, and also that it is particularly used with regard to the provision of medical services.

5   For a timeline of the key events in the case, see www.bbc.co.uk/news/
    uk-11626806
6   Estimated costs of principal tax reliefs from Gov.uk: https://assets.
    publishing.service.gov.uk/government/uploads/system/uploads/
    attachment_data/file/823739/Jan19_Principal_Reliefs_Final__Revised_
    for_Marriage_allowance.pdf
7   For more detail on the 100-day challenge, see www.nesta.org.uk/feature/
    six-initiatives-opening-health-innovation-around-world/people-powered-
    results/

Chapter 10

1   See for example the 2016 presentation by Health Education England:
    www.hee.nhs.uk/sites/default/files/documents/VBR_Framework%20
    March%202016.pdf
2   www.gov.uk/government/publications/open-academies-and-academy-
    projects-in-development
3   For a flavour of the arguments around academies and their impact, see
    www.theguardian.com/education/2018/jul/22/academy-schools-scandal-
    failing-trusts – for a different view from the government side: www.gov.
    uk/government/news/10-facts-you-need-to-know-about-academies
4   www.gov.uk/government/publications/social-investment-tax-relief-
    factsheet/social-investment-tax-relief
5   www.gov.uk/government/publications/social-value-act-information-and-
    resources/social-value-act-information-and-resources
6   https://gmsen.net/content/salford-social-enterprise-city
7   http://fairtradeamerica.org/Media-Center/Blog/2018/October/
    Fairtrade-tops-9-billion-in-global-sales

Chapter 11

1   For a simple introduction to the policy cycle, see Paul Cairney's blog:
    https://paulcairney.wordpress.com/2013/11/11/policy-concepts-in-1000-
    words-the-policy-cycle-and-its-stages/
2   https://www.ukri.org/news/pathways-to-impact-impact-core-to-the-uk-
    research-and-innovation-application-process/
3   The discussion was under the Chatham House Rule, so I am unable to give
    details that would identify the exact organisation concerned.
4   Michael Gove, interview on Sky News with Faisal Islam, 3 June 2016.
5   Tweet by Sajith Premasanda, 7 November 2019
6   Tweet by Sajith Premasanda, 9 October 2019. Many of the replies to this
    tweet made comments to the effect that it made no sense to ordinary voters.

References

Achen, C and Bartels, L (2016) *Democracy for Realists*, Princeton: Princeton University Press.

Adonis, A, Butler, D, and Travers, T (1994) *Failure in British Government: The Politics of the Poll Tax*, Oxford: Oxford University Press.

Alabrese, E, Becker, S, Fetzer, T and Novy, D (2019) 'Who voted for Brexit?', *European Journal of Political Economy* 56: 132–50.

Alesina, A and Fuchs-Schundeln, N (2006) 'Good bye Lenin (or not?): the effect of communism on people's preferences', Berkeley, CA: UC Berkeley, Institute of Governmental Studies, https://escholarship.org/uc/item/1tn2z0d1

Andre, K and Pache, A (2016) 'From caring entrepreneur to caring enterprise: addressing the ethical challenge of scaling up social enterprises', *Journal of Business Ethics* 133(4): 659–75.

Andrews, M (2013) 'How do governments get great?', discussion paper, Harvard Kennedy School.

Bagnera, E and Gagliani, M (2019) *Our Journey to the Shared Power Principle*, Centre for Public Impact, www.centreforpublicimpact.org/journey-shared-power-principle/

Baker, K (1978) 'French political thought at the accession of Louis XVI', *Journal of Modern History* 50(2): 279–303.

Barnea, M and Schwartz, S (1998) 'Values and voting', *Political Psychology* 19(1): 17–40.

Barnes, J (2010) 'From evidence-base to practice: implementation of the Nurse Family Partnership programme in England', *Journal of Children's Services* 5(4): 4–17.

Baumgartner, F and Jones, B (1993) *Agendas and Instability in American Politics*, Chicago, IL: University of Chicago Press.

Beck, EM and Tolney, SE (1995) *A Festival of Violence: An Analysis of Southern Lynchings, 1882–1930*, Chicago, IL: University of Illinois Press.

Blackburn, S (ed) (1994) *Oxford Dictionary of Philosophy*, Oxford, Oxford University Press.

Bradford, B (2017) *Stop and Search and Police Legitimacy*, London, Routledge.

Bryan, H and Revill, L (2016) 'Calibrating fundamental British values: how head teachers are approaching appraisal in the light of the Teachers' Standards 2012, Prevent and the Counter-Terrorism and Security Act, 2015', *Journal of Education for Teaching* 42(3): 341–53.

Burch, S and Smith, D (2008) 'Empty spaces and the value of symbols: Estonia's "war of monuments" from another angle', *Europe-Asia Studies* 59(6): 913–36.

Butler, D and Kavanagh, D (1984) *The British General Election of 1983*, London: Macmillan.

Cabinet Office (1999) *Modernising Government*, Command Paper 4310, London: The Stationery Office.

Cabinet Office (2018) *The What Works Network Five Years On*, London: Cabinet Office, www.gov.uk/government/publications/the-what-works-network-five-years-on

Cairney, P (2016) *The Politics of Evidence Based Policy Making*, London: Palgrave.

Cairney, P (2017) 'The politics of evidence based policy making', *Oxford Research Encyclopaedia of Policy-Making*, https://pdfs.semanticscholar.org/0fd2/cb18d42a2387b03a231b26520df913dfa70a.pdf

Cairney, P and Oliver, K (2017) 'Evidence based policy is not like evidence based medicine', *Health Research Policy and Systems* 15(35), https://health-policy-systems.biomedcentral.com/articles/10.1186/s12961-017-0192-x

Capara, G, Schwartz, S, Capanna, C, Vecchione, M and Barbaranelli, C (2006) 'Personality and politics: values, traits and political choice', *Political Psychology* 27(1): 1–28.

CBS (2017) 'Eight out of ten Americans think US will pay for the wall on southern border', https://www.cbsnews.com/news/eight-in-10-americans-think-u-s-will-pay-for-u-s-mexican-border-wall/

Centre for Public Impact (2018) *Finding a More Human Government*, London: Centre for Public Impact.

Chapman, C (2013) 'Academy federations, chains and teaching schools in England: reflections on leadership, policy and practice', *Journal of Education Policy* 7(3): 334–52.

Churchwell, S (2018) *Behold America: A History of America First and the American Dream*, London: Bloomsbury.

Corbacho, B, Bell, K, Stamuli, E, Richardson, G, Ronaldson, S, Hood, K, Sanders, J, Robling, M and Torgerson, D (2017) 'Cost-effectiveness of the Family Nurse Partnership (FNP) programme in England: Evidence from the building blocks trial', *Journal of Evaluation in Clinical Practice* 23(6): 1367–74.

Cottam, H (2018) *Radical Help*, London: Virago.

Crewe, I and King, A (2013) *Blunders of Our Governments*, London: OneWorld.

Daubler, T (2012) 'The preparation and use of election manifestos: learning from the Irish case', *Irish Political Studies* 27(1): 51–70.

Department for Education (2014) *Promoting Fundamental British Values through SMSC*, London: Department for Education.

DfES (Department for Education and Skills) (2005) *Higher Standards, Better Schools for All: More Choice for Parents and Pupils*, London: Department for Education and Skills.

Doig, A, Watt, D and Williams, R (2007) 'Why do developing country anti-corruption commissions fail to deal with corruption?', *Public Administration and Development* 27(3): 251–9.

Downs, A (1957) 'An economic theory of political action in a democracy', *Journal of Political Economy* 65(2): 135–50.

Dryzek, J (2002) *Deliberative Democracy and Beyond: Liberals, critics and contestations*, Oxford: Oxford University Press.

Edelman, M (1977) *Political Language: Words that Succeed and Policies that Fail*, New York: Institute for the Study of Poverty.

Edelman, M (1988) *Constructing the Political Spectacle*, Chicago, IL: University of Chicago Press.

Feldman, S and Stenner, K (1997) 'Perceived threat and authoritarianism', *Political Psychology* 18(4): 741–70.

Finlayson, L (2019) 'Short Cuts', *London Review of Books* 41(15): 10–11.

Foot, P (1967) 'The problem of abortion and the doctrine of double effect', *Oxford Review* 5.

Fukuyama, F (2014) *Political Order and Political Decay*, London: Profile.

Geertz, C (1973) *Interpretation of Cultures*, New York: Basic.

Gemperle, S (2018) 'Comparing anti-corruption agencies: a new cross-national index', *International Review of Public Administration* 23(3): 156–75.

Goldstein, A (2017) *Janesville: An American Story*, New York: Simon & Schuster.

Gray, P and Timmins, N (2018) *Reforming Working-Age Social Security: Lessons for Policy-Makers*, London: Institute for Government.

Gunther, B (2015) 'Do we remember much from television news?', in *The Cognitive Impact of Television News*, London: Palgrave Macmillan.

Haidt, J (2012) *The Righteous Mind*, London: Penguin.

Hallsworth, M, Egan, M, Rutter, J and McCrea, J (2018) *Behavioural Government*, London: Institute for Government.

Hampton, A (2006) *Local Government and Investment Promotion in China*, Brighton: Institute of Development Studies.

Hanson, P and Teague, E (2005) 'Big business and the state in Russia', *Euro-Asia Studies* 57(5): 657–80.

Hardman, K and Naul, R (2002) 'Sport and physical education in the two Germanies 1945–1990', in Hardman, K and Naul, R (eds) *Sport and Physical Education in Germany*, London: Taylor and Francis.

Hayek, F (1944) *The Road to Serfdom*, London: Routledge.

Heald, D (1988) 'The United Kingdom: privatisation and its political context', *West European Politics* 11(4): 31–48.

Helm, D and Jenkinson, T (1997) 'The assessment: introducing competition into regulated industries', *Oxford Review of Economic Policy* 13(1): 1–13.

Hill, S (2014) 'Low voter turnout in Police and Crime Commissioner elections in England and Wales: how it can be addressed', University of East Anglia Politics Department blog, www.ueapolitics.org/2014/03/25/low-voter-turnout-at-police-and-crime-commissioner-elections/

HM Government (2010) *The Coalition: Our Programme for Government*, London: HM Government, https://assets. publishing.service.gov.uk/government/uploads/system/ uploads/attachment_data/file/78977/coalition_programme_ for_government.pdf

HM Government (2013) *The Coalition: Together in the National Interest – Mid Term Review*, London: HM Government, www. gov.uk/government/publications/the-coalition-government-mid-term-review/the-coalition-together-in-the-national-interest-mid-term-review

House of Commons Treasury Select Committee (2008) *The Run on the Rock: Fifth Report of Session 2007–08. Volume I: Report, together with formal minutes*, London: Stationery Office, https://publications.parliament.uk/pa/cm200708/cmselect/ cmtreasy/56/56i.pdf

Inglehart, R and Norris, P (2016) 'Trump, Brexit and the rise of populism', working paper, Harvard Kennedy School.

Inglehart, R and Norris, P (2018) *Cultural Backlash: Trump, Brexit and the Rise of Authoritarian Populism*, Cambridge: Cambridge University Press.

Institute for Fiscal Studies (1997) *What Explains Support for Higher Public Spending*, London: Institute for Fiscal Studies.

Institute of Development Studies (2010) *An Upside-Down View of Governance*, Brighton: Institute of Development Studies.

Iversen, T and Soskice, D (2019) *Democracy and Prosperity: Reinventing Capitalism through a Turbulent Century*, Princeton, NJ: Princeton University Press.

Jennings, W and Stoker, G (2016) 'The bifurcation of politics: two Englands', *Political Quarterly* 87(3): 372–82.

Jennings, W and Stoker, G (2017) 'Tilting towards the cosmopolitan axis', *Political Quarterly* 88(3): 359–69.

John, P (1998) *Analysing Public Policy*, London: Continuum.

Jordan, E (2019) 'Boston Mayor's Office of New Urban Mechanics', case study for the Centre for Public Impact, www. centreforpublicimpact.org/case-study/bostons-mayors-office-new-urban-mechanics/

Jump, R and Michell, J (2020) *Deprivation and the Electoral Geography of Brexit*, www.researchgate.net/publication/339090435_ Deprivation_and_the_electoral_geography_of_Brexit

Kahan, D, Peters, E, Dawson, E and Slovic, P (2017) 'Motivated numeracy and enlightened self-government', *Behavioural Public Policy* 1(01): 54–86.

Kahneman, D and Tversky, A (1974) 'Judgements under uncertainty: heuristics and biases', *Science* 185(4157): 1124–31.

Katayama, S and Ursprung, H (2004) 'Commercial culture, political culture and economic policy polarization: The case of Japan', *Journal of Economic Behaviour and Organisation* 54(3): 351–75.

Katznelson, I (2013) *Fear Itself: The New Deal and the Origins of Our Time*, New York: Norton.

Kaufman, E (2017) 'Values and immigration: the real reasons behind Brexit and Trump', in Main, J, Clark, T, Fowler, N, Snoddy, R and Tait, R (eds) *Brexit, Trump and the Media*, Bury St Edmunds: Abramis.

Kelly, G, Muers, S and Mulgan, G (2002) 'Creating public value: an analytical framework for public service reform', discussion paper, London: Cabinet Office.

Ken, J, Derek, E, Colclough, S and Williamson, S (2010) *Review into the Four Hour Emergency Access Reporting at Nottingham University Hospital Final Report*, Somerset: Deardon Consulting.

Key, VO (1949) *Southern Politics in State and Nation*, Knoxville, TN: University of Tennessee Press.

King, D (2006) *Fiscal Autonomy of Sub-Central Governments*, Paris: OECD.

Kingdon, J (1984) *Agendas, Alternatives and Public Policies*, New York: HarperCollins.

Knowles, E (2006) *What They Didn't Say: A Book of Misquotations*, Oxford: Oxford University Press.

Kramer, K (2016) *The Politics of Resentment*, Chicago, IL: University of Chicago Press.

Labour Party (2017) *For the Many, Not the Few*, https://labour.org.uk/wp-content/uploads/2017/10/labour-manifesto-2017.pdf

LaMay, C (1997) 'America's censor: Anthony Comstock and free speech', *Communications and the Law* 1.

Lander, V (2016) 'Introduction', special edition, *Journal of Education for Teaching* 42(3): 274–9.

Lewin, R (2002) 'Investigating the benefits of mutuality: a discussion of the demutualisation trend', *Journal of Pensions Management* 7(4): 313–36.

Lipsky, M (1979) *Street-Level Bureaucracy*, New York: Russell Sage.

Ma (2017) *In Search of a Better Chinese Language Policy: A Comparative Study Between China's Case and France's Case*, discussion paper, Paris: University of Sorbonne.

Marquette University Poll in Wisconsin (2017) Reported at https://law.marquette.edu/poll/wp-content/uploads/2017/03/MLSP42Instrument.pdf

Marshall, J, Pike, A, Pollard, J, Tomaney, J, Dawley, S and Gray, J (2012) 'Placing the run on Northern Rock', *Journal of Economic Geography* 12: 157–81.

McAndrew, S, O'Brien, D and Taylor, M (2019) 'The values of culture? Social closure in the political identities, policy preferences and social attitudes of cultural and creative workers', *Sociological Review* 67.

McCrae, R and John, O (1992) 'An introduction to the five-factor model and its applications' *Journal of Personality* 60: 175–216

Moore, GE (1903) *Principia Ethica*, Cambridge: Cambridge University Press.

Muers, S (2004) 'Deliberative democracy and urban regeneration: justification and evaluation', *Public Policy and Administration* 19(4): 34–56.

Muers, S (2017) 'Talking about ethics in impact investing', *Stanford Social Innovation Review*, https://ssir.org/articles/entry/talking_about_ethics_in_impact_investing

Muers, S (2019) 'How Donald Trump shows us the future', in *Radical Visions of a Future Government*, London: Nesta.

Murray, R (1976) *The 103rd Ballot: Democrats and the Disaster in Madison Square Gardens*, New York: Harper.

Murrell, P (1993) 'What is shock therapy? What did it do in Poland and Russia?' *Post-Soviet Affairs* 9(2): 111–40.

Myddelton, D (2014) 'The British approach to privatisation', *Economic Affairs* 34(2): 129–38.

NAO (National Audit Office) (2006) *Child Support Agency: Implementation of the Child Support Reforms*, London: National Audit Office.

NAO (2009) *The Department for Transport: The Failure of Metronet*, London: National Audit Office.

NAO (2013) *Responding to Changes in Jobcentres*, London: National Audit Office.

NAO (2019) *Transforming Rehabilitation: Progress Review*, London: National Audit Office.

Naurin, E (2011) *Election Promises, Party Behaviour and Voter Perceptions*, Basingstoke: Macmillan.

Nesta (2019a) *Public Value: How can it be Measured, Managed and Grown*, London: Nesta.

Nesta (2019b) *20 Tools for Innovating in Government*, London: Nesta.

Olds, D (2006) 'The nurse–family partnership: an evidence based intervention', *Infant Mental Health Journal* 27(1).

Ostrom, E (2000) 'Collective action and the evolution of social norms', *The Journal of Economic Perspectives* (14)3: 137–58.

Ostrom, E (2009) 'Beyond markets and states: polycentric governance of complex economic systems', Nobel Prize acceptance lecture, www.nobelprize.org/uploads/2018/06/ostrom_lecture.pdf

Page, E (2016) 'What's methodology got to do with it?: Public policy, observational analysis and RCTs', in Keman, H and Woldendorp, JJ (eds) *Handbook of Research Methods and Applications in Political Science*, Cheltenham: Edward Elgar, pp 483–96.

Patunru, AA, McCullogh, N and Von Lubke, C (2009) *A Tale of Two Cities: The Political Economy of the Investment Climate in Solo and Manado, Indonesia*, Brighton: Institute for Development Studies.

Parsons, W (2001) *Public Policy* (revised edition), Cheltenham: Edward Elgar.

Parsons, W (2002) 'From muddling through to muddling up: evidence based policy-making and the modernisation of British government', *Public Policy and Administration*, 17(3): 43–60.

Populus (2018a) 'The political stories that the public really notice', www.populus.co.uk/insights/2018/04/the-political-stories-that-the-public-really-notice/

Populus (2018b) 'Brexit tops the news agenda – but it doesn't mean people are interested', www.populus.co.uk/insights/2018/12/brexit-tops-the-news-agenda-but-it-doesnt-mean-people-are-interested/

PriceWaterhouseCoopers (2017) *Effectiveness of Tax Incentives for Venture Capital and Business Angels to Foster the Investment of SMEs and Start-Ups*, Brussels: European Commission.

Public Management Foundation (1996) *The Glue That Binds: Public Value of Public Services*, London: Public Management Foundation and MORI.

Putnam, R (1993) *Making Democracy Work: Civic Traditions in Modern Italy*, Princeton, NJ: Princeton University Press.

Puttick, R and Ludlow, J (2013) *Standards of Evidence*, London: Nesta.

Qian, Y (2003) 'How reform worked in China' in Rodrik, D (ed) *In Search of Prosperity. Analytic Narratives on Economic Growth*, Princeton, NJ: Princeton University Press.

Rhodes, R (1997) *Understanding Governance: Policy Networks, Governance, Reflexivity and Accountability*, Milton Keynes: Open University Press.

Rhu, S-R (2017) 'Promises are promises? A study of campaign promise fulfilment among South Korean legislators, 2008–2012', *Korea Journal* 57(1): 65–89.

Richards, S (2019) *The Prime Ministers: Reflections on Leadership from Wilson to May*, London: Atlantic Books.

Robling, M et al (2016) 'Effectiveness of a nurse-led intensive home-visitation programme for first-time teenage mothers (Building Blocks): a pragmatic randomised controlled trial', *The Lancet* 387(10014): 146–55.

Rodden, J (2009) 'Socialist heroes in East German schoolbooks', *Society* 46(2): 168–74.

Sabatier, P and Jenkins-Smith, H (1999) 'The Advocacy Coalition Framework – an assessment', in Sabatier, P (ed) *Theories of the Policy Process*, Boulder, CO: Westview Press.

Samy, L (2012) 'Extending home ownership before the First World War: the case of the Co-Operative Permanent Building Society 1884–1913', *The Economic History Review* 65(1): 168–93.

Sandel, M (2005) *Public Philosophy: Essays on Morality in Politics*, Cambridge, MA: Harvard University Press.

Sandel, M (2009) 'Morality in Politics', BBC Reith Lecture.

Scharf, CB (1988) 'Social policy and social conditions in the GDR', *International Institute of Sociology* 18(3): 3–24.

Schwartz, S (1992) 'Universals in the content and structure of values: Theoretical advances and empirical tests in 20 countries', in Zanna, M (ed) *Advances in Experimental Social Psychology*, New York: Academic Press.

Scott, P and Newton, L (2012) 'Advertising and promotion: the rise of a national building society movement in inter-war Britain', *Journal of Business History* 54(3): 399–423.

Service, R (2007) *Comrades! A World History of Communism*, Basingstoke: Macmillan.

Shah, A (2007) *Participatory Budgeting*, Washington DC: The World Bank Group.

Simon, H (1997) *Models of Bounded Rationality: Empirically Grounded Economic Reason*, Boston, MA: MIT Press.

Social Finance (2019) *Investing in the Enablers of Local Integrated Care*, discussion paper, London: Social Finance, www.socialfinance.org.uk/sites/default/files/publications/investing_in_the_enablers_of_local_integrated_care.pdf

Stenner, K (2005) *The Authoritarian Dynamic*, Cambridge: Cambridge University Press.

Sumner, C, Scofield, J, Buchanan, E, Evans, M and Shearing, M (2018) *Personality, Authoritarianism, Numeracy, Thinking Styles and Cognitive Biases in the UK's 2016 Referendum on EU Membership*, working paper, Online Privacy Foundation, www.researchgate.net/publication/326163776_The_Role_of_Personality_Authoritarianism_and_Cognition_in_the_United_Kingdom's_2016_Referendum_on_European_Union_Membership

Thapa, B (1999) 'Environmentalism: The relation of environmental attitudes and environmentally responsible behaviors among undergraduate students', *Bulletin of Science, Technology and Society* 19(5): 426–38.

Vance, J (2016) *Hillbilly Elegy: A Memoir of a Family and a Culture in Crisis*, New York: Harper.

Veron, P (2018) 'Participatory Paris: home of the largest participatory budget in the world', *Royal Society of Arts Journal* 3, https://medium.com/rsa-journal/participatory-paris-home-of-the-largest-participatory-budget-in-the-world-37425aab9a99

Ware, A (1996) *Political Parties and Party Systems*, Oxford: Oxford University Press.

Weber, M (1978) *Economy and Society*, Berkeley, CA: University of California Press.

Whelan, E (2018) 'An All-Ireland Win for abortion law reform', *Conscience* 39(2): 1.

Wodak, R (2015) *The Politics of Fear: What Right-Wing Populist Discourse Means*, London: Sage.

Woods, P, Woods, G and Gunther, H (2007) 'Academy schools and entrepreneurialism in education', *Journal of Education Policy* 22(2): 237–59.

World Bank (2008a) *Toward a More Inclusive and Effective Participatory Budget in Porto Alegre: Volume 1*, Washington DC: World Bank Group.

World Bank (2008b) *Public Sector Reform: What Works and Why?* Washington DC: World Bank Group.

Yakovlev, A (2006) 'The evolution of business–state interaction in Russia – from state capture to business capture?', *Euro-Asia Studies* 58(7): 1033–56

Young, A (2005) *Judging the Image: Art, Value, Law*, London: Routledge.

Young, K and Mason, C (1983) 'The significance of urban programmes' in Young, K and Mason, C (eds) *Urban Economic Development: New Roles and Relationships*, London: Macmillan.

Index